I0390462

Lessons in Leadership

Taking Responsibility:
Heart, Mind and Soul

Jeff Hamill

Copyright © 2019 by Jeffrey S. Hamill

Registration number TXu 2-163-388

All rights reserved.

ISBN: 13-9781097332717

Imprint: Independently published

Website: jhleadership.com

CONTENTS

Foreword

Taking Responsibility: Heart, Mind and Soul

It gives me immense pleasure and pride to be writing this foreword for Jeff Hamill. I am thrilled that Jeff is sharing his knowledge, experiences and ways of thinking that will allow others to grow as leaders - both at work and beyond. Jeff is as authentic as they come. He's a superior person; a fearless and courageous leader. His thirst to learn and passion to teach makes him an ideal person to write this book to help others in their life journey.

My relationship with Jeff goes back to our Starbucks days. As the head of the company's largest operating division Jeff was my first external executive hire. He was selected to lead one of the highest growth markets in all of Starbucks. Jeff was a perfect fit with our unique culture. He valued serving people and driving superior performance. He was a disciplined operator with a willingness to learn, follow and teach the Starbucks processes and systems to enable the consistent delivery of the Starbucks Experience across a growing network of stores. Finally, he fully embraced Starbucks Culture and Core Purpose. He did everything necessary to mobilize his team, from the baristas on the front-line to the Partners in the Regional Offices, to understand and live our Mission Statement and Guiding Principles.

As a "Blue Chip" Leader he added value and made an immediate impact. His business unit often led Starbucks other twelve US Regions in same store sales and net profit growth. I still smile when I think about Jeff encouraging his team at a large conference - *"I see double-digit growth as far as the eye can see."* While the team didn't always get there, he never failed to set high expectations. Due to his Region's sustained success, Jeff was selected as the VP of Operations for Mainland China. Working with the Greater China team, Jeff was instrumental in helping set global strategy and in developing the Starbucks business in mainland China. I couldn't have been prouder.

In *Taking Responsibility: Heart, Mind and Soul* Jeff shares real life lessons from his long and distinguished leadership career. It is a compilation of proven practices, pragmatic methods and experiences related to business leadership. There is something here for everyone - whether you are just starting out, or you're a Senior Executive.

I personally benefited from Jeff's mentoring during our time at Starbucks. As a *"Heart Guy"*, with a strong people bias, I sometimes struggled with holding under-performers accountable. Jeff must have been thinking about me when he wrote "Accountability of

Results" in Chapter Five. As usual, Jeff speaks the truth and pulls no punches when he says:

"Poor performance in measurable results should never be rationalized or excused away by responsible leaders. There should be no excuses, ever. Taking responsibility…. for below par results and having a genuine sense of urgency to modify direction and mobilize the team to act is the hallmark of a good leader."

Jeff's mentoring and example helped me to be a better person and more responsible leader.

What you will learn from Jeff is the importance of spending your time on those things that matter most. With that in mind I wanted to highlight two core areas, Leading People and Managing the Core Business, as they distinguish high performing organizations.

Leading People: Jeff understands sustainable success in business is having a flow of the right people on the team who are the right culture fit. Jeff shares the proven methods, practices and experiences that need to be in place to develop a highly effective team of people. You'll walk away understanding Strategic Talent Management as an everyday priority. Jeff *"connects the dots"* on recruiting, selecting for fit, hiring, training, communication and rewarding your people to foster a Performance Driven Team Culture.

I'll never forget Jeff's presentation of his Region's team

at a U.S. Retail Succession Planning Meeting in Seattle. He showcased his people and their talents at a depth of knowledge that was flawless. Jim Donald, our CEO, was in attendance. He was blown away by Jeff's command of his people. I remember him blurting out - *"How do you know all of this?"* The answer is quite simple. Growing a high performing team was Jeff's top priority, His calendar reflected it. The quality of his thinking on people development was always current. He was active in Group Interviews and Succession Planning meetings. He stayed connected to the top talent in his Region. Leaders often *"talk the talk"* while Jeff walked the talk. That's why his region was always fully staffed. He had a pipeline of talent to support future growth and he was an exporter of talent for the company. That discipline served as a model for others and hopefully his wisdom will help to do the same for you.

Managing the Core Business: Jeff provides for us a true understanding of how a business works. He moves beyond the *"smart talk,"* and into the guts of how a business really comes to life. You will be coached by a leader who is not afraid to roll up his sleeves and dig deep for the answers to the big questions that need to be asked: How does the business work? What factual data and expert analysis is needed for better decision making? What is critical to the customer experience? What are your core processes and how do you make them a fabric of your business culture? He is a *"Living in the Basics"* leader and is relentless in creating a culture of responsibility.

After joining Starbucks Jeff helped the company's growth by infusing the discipline, structure and matters of the "mind" he learned during his career at 7-Eleven. He strengthened the Starbucks culture by blending the Starbucks values with the development skills of business basics. He was tireless in reinforcing the message of *"Living in the Basics"* and the use of existing tools and resources to deliver on our core processes - store cleanliness, beverage quality, speed of service. He would often end his message with what has become a long remembered *"Jeff-ism:"*

"When you live relentlessly in the basics you will never go back to the basics. It's like brushing your teeth."

There was a defining moment when you knew that his team had embraced his *"Living in the Basics"* message. It was the day his team presented him with a giant toothbrush that signaled their trust in his message and belief in him as their leader.

Jeff placed a *Big Bet* on the belief that a discipline of repeatable routines, done as a team, was the right way to better serve the customer and create competitive advantage. The bet paid off - and I know it could for others as well.

I write this with my high hopes that Jeff's work will

influence others to lead responsibly, to allow them to grow as leaders and to accomplish their goals.

Mark Lindstrom - Seven Lakes West, North Carolina
June – 2019

Introduction

Taking Responsibility: Heart, Mind and Soul

Taking Responsibility: Heart, Mind and Soul is primarily a compilation of techniques, methods and experiences related to business leadership.

The perspective is from a mid-level to senior leadership in a multiple store, corporate environment that examines proven processes and disciplines. This writing is practical and real.

Many of the values discussed are rooted in my upbringing led by a single mom, and three influential brothers. My sense of being is about *taking responsibility* for big and small things.

My mom was my first example of courageous leadership, *taking responsibility* through severe economic and personal challenges to nurture, educate and support four young boys from a "broken home."

Consequently, my three brothers and me, facing the same hardships as my mom, embraced the responsibility for each other to support and lead with love and courage. This mutual support and leadership with courage and love have led to all highly successful marriages, families and careers.

My mom's legacy of support, love and courageous leadership is alive today through her 8 grandchildren, and *now* through 15 great grandchildren all born after her passing. The key work and life learning from my mom and brothers are that by overcoming obstacles and rejecting being a victim in any circumstance, success will ultimately reign. It is the core of *taking responsibility*.

Heart, mind and soul is about putting every part of one's being into owning, caring and striving for excellence. This writing will provide examples of these pivotal aspects of *taking responsibility* at work and in life outside of work.

Heart relates to the power, energy and magic of people and team and how that relates to performance and results.

Mind relates to smart action that properly leads, directs and secures a path to success based on facts and proven methods.

Soul relates to culture, character and the guiding values of the leader and the team and how to sustain that purpose.

My goal in writing this book is to share experiences and learnings to help others deal with adversity, use facts in making decisions, communicate effectively and be accountable for performance & results.

Chapter One
Career Journey

My work career actually started in 1964 when I delivered Los Angeles Herald Examiner newspapers on my bicycle to about 40 homes each day including Sunday. I mention this, as I gained a sense of responsibility at 9 years of age until age 16 to fulfill duties of serving customers and collecting monthly fees for services rendered. This was a valuable and practical experience that prepared me for every subsequent job responsibility or position I held over the next 45 years.

In high school and throughout college, I worked at Kentucky Fried Chicken, Shell service stations and Sears Roebuck stores all of which provided invaluable experience in product preparation, communication and customer service. This spanned over 9 years delivering product services in mostly retail-oriented, customer-facing roles. The experience gained in these positions spurred my subsequent career with 4 major multi-facility organizations over nearly 36 years. Taking Responsibility for me was born early and sustains to this day in heart, mind and soul.

The "Sheepskin"

Though, and because, my mom did not have a college

degree, she encouraged us throughout our years in school to strive to achieve that "sheepskin." I learned what that meant very early on. As you may know, "sheepskin" is a term for a college diploma. In past generations, the material or parchment used for diplomas came from sheepskin. I doubt that is the case in 2019, or even, 1981. However, it was my mom's way of creating a memorable reminder that a college diploma is something that is a standard of expectation. This mindset of mentoring key sustainable ways to take responsibility for life and prosperity is a life gift from my mom and my family.

My 3 brothers each graduated from college in four years or less. That was not the case with me. I was on a much longer path to that accomplishment. I attended 3 Junior Colleges and 4 upper division colleges until I finally graduated from St. Mary's College in Moraga, California in 1981, eight years after I graduated from high school. Simply, after a very average academic performance in high school, I was not prepared to perform in college immediately afterwards. My lack of readiness was due to immaturity, and thus, lack of commitment. Changing colleges and meandering through different curriculums until the age of 22 only yielded a 2-year Associate of Arts degree from Diablo Valley College in Pleasant Hill, California in 1977. Though I worked full-time and lived on my own from age 20, there was no excuse or reason, other than immaturity, for my lack of academic performance.

In 1979, I married my wife Kathy and started my career in multi-facility retail. A year later, Kathy was pregnant with my son Dan. With a baby and more responsibility on the way, I suddenly had the desire and drive to finish what I started with achieving my bachelor's degree, mainly because my new family created desire I had not felt before. With the help of my company, 7-Eleven, I enrolled in a night degree program at St. Mary's College to achieve a bachelor's degree in management. Thankfully, I had successfully lobbied my boss for an educational support initiative and that helped with my tuition. That boss, Pat Lawson, became my mentor as a part of the program requirement at St. Mary's. I am grateful to Pat for his personal time investment, and for garnering approval of the company, as it eased the financial burden we really could not afford. In less than 2 years, I was able to successfully complete my bachelor's degree in September 1981.

My mom and family were able to celebrate this achievement with me. For her, she had 4 sons with a "sheepskin" and she once again succeeded in the guidance she provided to each of us. All 3 of my brothers, as well as, other family members attended the graduation at the beautiful St. Mary's campus. My confidence, sense of responsibility and new maturity were all enriched. And, mom was right. The degree delivered as a ticket to entry for positions I competed for over my career. *Taking responsibility* for life and career in heart, mind and soul paid off after significant adversity in the process. I still wear my St. Mary's college ring daily as a reminder of the hard work and difficult path I endured to reach this important goal.

7-Eleven Convenience Stores

My leadership career at 7-Eleven (at that time Southland Corporation) started in 1979. The journey included fourteen different positions over twenty-two years. I was engaged in the business from entry level store operations to top level senior management at company headquarters. Though I had three more stops at other companies over the next fourteen years, my affinity and heart will always be with 7-Eleven, where "taking responsibility" was encased and forged in my being.

Most of my career at 7-Eleven was devoted to franchise operations where I led small sub-groups that progressed to Districts, Markets and Zones and ultimately to Regional Divisions with as many as 750 7-Eleven stores. Additionally, I had several merchandising leadership positions in operating Divisions eventually leading to my appointment in merchandising leadership at the headquarters in Dallas. I worked with some outstanding people in the west coast divisions that supported in my leadership. I am grateful for the learning and support from corporate leaders and the many franchisees I had the privilege to serve as a leader and colleague.

There are several leaders I worked for at 7-Eleven that provided significant mentorship, direction and guidance that were skilled, and at times, brilliant in their business management and leadership. The very long list of people that had lasting impact on my career development cannot be captured in this writing as I would not want to exclude anyone. Division Managers, Zone Managers, District Managers and countless others contributed greatly to my development over the 2 decades with the company. Many of the experiences related to business leadership in this writing come from these people.

The unique opportunity to lead the company's category management, merchandising department & process in Dallas headquarters provided excellent insight for me with product decisions impacting 7500 stores. This is where I gained broad experience in senior leadership of key functions and serving great people that do exceptional work on a daily basis with a multi-national convenience store company. The learning to get things done by syncing with numerous functional leaders was invaluable and consequential in my experience.

I am grateful to Jim Keyes, the CEO of 7-Eleven

Incorporated in 1998, for the trust and confidence to appoint me to Vice President of the Southwest Division for 7-Eleven Incorporated. In 2000 he doubled down by bringing me to headquarters for a broader role. This period was pivotal in my development and joy as a leader. I will never forget the great people around me in support with the leaders, colleagues, franchisees and the teams I served.

Swifty Serve Convenience Stores

One of my most difficult and dubious career decisions occurred when I left 7-Eleven in 2002 to become President and CEO of a 500-store convenience store chain called Swifty Serve headquartered in North Carolina. I was intrigued by the opportunity to take on complete responsibility for the business organization reporting to a board of private investors. My enthusiasm in heart, mind and soul for the opportunity to take responsibility at the highest level of the company was overwhelming. Unfortunately, I quickly discovered that leading Swifty Serve was not about the customer or operating business but to negotiate with creditors, investors and lenders to salvage a debt-ridden and cash hemorrhaging chain of stores. I anticipated some of this, but the degree of the problem was suffocating. The bills weren't getting paid and the very fatigued investor group had little appetite and patience to invest further.

My tenure lasted only 5 months, leading to the last act as senior leader taking responsibility in heart, mind and soul in ensuring the 3200 employees were paid for the time they worked. The company was forced into Chapter 11 bankruptcy on Friday, October 4, 2002. My greatest concern was for the people that spent many years at Swifty Serve with dedicated service. It was not their fault that very poor financial decisions were made over a long period of years that proved fatal for the enterprise. I wanted so much to help turn the company around and reward each employee with success that matched their loyalty and hard work. Unfortunately, that was never going to occur.

Dealing with the serious adversity of my move to Swifty Serve taught me extremely important lessons. I was impulsive, over-confident and naive in my judgment of the situation with the company when I accepted the CEO position. There were many red flags that I failed to consider in my assessment of the company, not the least of which included negative cash and high debt. In retrospect, though I now know the prospects of success at Swifty were dismal, I learned that skepticism and detailed analysis with reliance on expert advice is imperative in considering new endeavors and responsibilities. This was the lowest point of my career, and I have carried this learning with me for the nearly 20 years since.

Starbucks Coffee Company

The next phase: I was fortunate to join Starbucks in Southern California almost immediately after leaving Swifty Serve in the fall of 2002. The Starbucks role included operating responsibility for 350 stores in Los Angeles as Region Vice President. This was at a time when store growth was at a very robust pace for the company. During this period, my position was one of thirteen in the North American business, and the culture and personal growth opportunity was unbelievable. In nearly 7 years, I had the awesome opportunity to work twice, two different periods, with teams in Southern California that grew to over 600 stores from 2002 to 2008.

Starbucks was an organization focused on "heart." After spending 22 years with 7-Eleven with a heavy dose of operational standards and understanding the numbers, it was clear my contribution would be needed to help the chain grow using discipline, structure and matters of the "mind." We were very successful and built a strong team of leaders with the values of Starbucks balanced with the developing skills of business basics to achieve results effectively and efficiently. Our Region often led Starbucks in same store sales growth and net profit compared to the other 12 North American regions. It was a great run of performance.

With this success of the Region team, I was privileged and honored to be selected to live and work in Shanghai, China for 18 months as the Operations Vice President, working with the Greater China team. This period was prior to the Beijing Olympics, and a key part of our objectives related to helping the global strategy come to reality. We were pioneers in developing the Starbucks business in mainland China- the richest experience in my entire career. We also led the existing business and stores with joint venture/licensed partners in Taiwan and Hong Kong. Starbucks continues to be a world class organization, with the emphasis on class. The whole time with Starbucks was energizing and inspiring to me, as I was able to work beside great people in a company with exceptional values.

It's difficult to name everyone because there are so many, but there were, and there are, incredible people at Starbucks. My first team at Starbucks was small but powerful. Shelli Taylor and Tesh Burke grew up with the company and provided significant support to me in immersing into the Starbucks culture. The guide path and welcome for the "convenience store guy" was instrumental in my early sense of belonging and success in building our team. Sarah Rogers and her boss Cindy Chrispell are excellent and talented Human Resources professionals that supported our essential people development mission. I will always hold these folks in high esteem and was fortunate to be associated with them.

With my return from China and back into the North American business, I will always be grateful for the strong leadership of Cos LaPorta. We were colleagues for several years and our partnership in addressing challenges while working under his leadership in Southern California during the 2008 period has had lasting impact. I have great respect for Cos as a person and a leader.

Smile Brands Dental Service Organization

In 2009, after a 6 ½ year run as a Region Vice President, I made the decision to leave Starbucks. My leadership experience was greatly enhanced at Starbucks, and I loved my team in Southern California after returning from an exciting role in China. However, I still yearned to lead at a higher level with broader responsibility. There were many changes going on inside of Starbucks, at the time, that did not indicate a clear view for me in my desire to grow and have a bigger impact in the organization.

During the time working in China, I was diagnosed with Non-Hodgkins Lymphoma, which shortened a 3-year commitment to 18 months. The company was outstanding in support of me returning to the US for surgery, treatment and recovery. I was thankful to return to my former role in Southern California after treatment and made progress in the health prognosis;

however, this health crisis, in my mind, interrupted momentum in my desire to lead at a higher level. The China role was preparatory for positions leading larger teams and business units and the mission was interrupted. In retrospect, I was impatient and itching to get back on track at Starbucks.

The call came from Smile Brands (formerly Bright Now! Dental). I met with Steve Bilt, the CEO, and developed a good connection in multiple meetings. I felt his potential mentorship in this new sector for me would be valuable should I decide to make the change. I also saw an opportunity to grow as a senior leader to a more enterprise-wide role with the company and serve a larger group. The company headquarters was located in Southern California nearby my home. With this all considered, I accepted the role with Smile Brands, with the idea that I had a better chance to broaden my swath of leadership to serve others.

With nearly 7 years at Smile Brands, I saw many changes, some positive, and some that proved flawed and nearly fatal for the enterprise. But, importantly, I loved my team and we achieved a tremendous amount of growth and success together. No matter what was going on with the company, our doctors and office teams developed their leadership skills and showed daily improvement in the patient care basics. In the face of extraordinary adversity, our team delivered and did so with hard work and high energy in heart, mind and soul. At no time was there a "woe is me" attitude of despair.

In retrospect, though I am very proud of the work, results and relationships developed at Smile Brands, there were likely better avenues to achieve my personal career goals and actually broaden my leadership swath at this stage of my journey. Nonetheless, I have no regrets as career goals are not equal to taking responsibility in heart, mind and soul and helping others achieve *their* goals. I appreciate and grew personally from the Smile Brands experience, and my rich relationships with my operating team while serving dentists and staffs so well and teaching me so much in the dental sector.

<u>Red Mango Franchise</u>

In 2013, along with my wife Kathy, we purchased a yogurt, smoothie and juice bar store in Los Angeles. We thought it would be fun and exciting to serve customers and employees in an enterprise we owned and developed. With this, while I worked at Smile Brands to finish what I started, Kathy took full control of the daily operation from October 2013 until January 2016 when I joined her. She did a great job before and after I entered the business full time.

We had a lot of fun together, and I probably learned more from her than vice versa in handling modern employee issues, which are constant. It was, at times challenging, but at the same time, very rewarding in owning and managing this small business in partnership with my wife Kathy. We sold the business in 2018 after nearly 5 years of operation. We are proud that we took responsibility in heart, mind and soul for the young people who worked with us, the great customers we served and the brand we stewarded.

Perspective

My career in retail, food service and healthcare multi-store management and leadership over 35 years has been challenging, energizing and extremely fulfilling. I was able to apply everything I learned from my less than privileged up-bringing. I built a new confidence at Diablo Valley College and St. Mary's College after a slow start to my post-high school academic career. And, importantly, 7-Eleven, Swifty Serve, Starbucks, Smile Brands and Red Mango all contributed to provide the real-life lessons in taking responsibility in heart, mind and soul that I have carried with me.

Many years ago, early in my career, I had a leader coach me that it is more important to *be good* rather than *look good*. I found incredible wisdom in that statement. To me, the best measure of being good is how one overcomes adversity and prospers, while having the humility to admit mistakes honestly. My career has had many high points as well as a good number of low points, but the hard work, the thoughtful plan and the drive to succeed has never changed. With this, taking responsibility in heart, mind and soul is fundamentally about *being good* not just *looking good* or how others perceive you. The trend of objective performance measures defines *being good* in my experience. We maximized our production at every juncture with every team over my career.

Finally, in General Colin Powell's *Leadership Primer,* he describes "Perpetual optimism as a force multiplier" in Lesson 12. I firmly embrace General Powell's assertion. Throughout this writing you will discover that my experience, learning and action is fueled by this attitude. Great leaders believe in their mission, their people and themselves in planning and executing with a sense of enthusiasm and optimism.

Chapter Two

<u>Leading People (Heart)</u>

The overwhelming priority of success in business and pretty much anything we face in life is the importance of people and having the connection to the magic of talent and energy around us. It has been a privilege in my experience to witness some outstanding leadership coming from people I have worked with and worked for. There have been some very hard times and some very exhilarating times in this process, but through the best and the worst of times, lessons in leadership always showed through.

I will always remember the business courses in college highlighting the fundamentals of "managing people." This approach framed managers as "task-oriented" or "people-oriented." Much of this was compartmentalized and the takeaway was that a manager was pretty much one or the other. Though these studies occurred in the mid to late 1970's, naïve folks like me, at the time, sort of booked it as gospel.

The main point of business training in college that doesn't seem to have translated to the reality of business is that leadership and management are different. Great leaders are generally top-flight managers, but great managers are not always exceptional leaders. Being "people oriented" was once looked at as soft and maybe weak in in terms of being able to command a team. The opposite is true. Having strong connections and the magic of listening to and caring about people creates strength in command. This is fundamental to taking responsibility.

This is not to say strong management skills are unimportant in the leader or the team. The ability to manage key facets of business are technical skills that are developed and come from experience and talent. Strong people skills, which are somewhat intrinsic, married with strong management skills which are largely learned, enable the individual to be on the senior leader track.

At Starbucks, there was such a commitment to connecting with people that senior leaders, selected strategically, came together off-site for a workshop called "Leading from the Heart." The then Chairman & CEO of Starbucks, Howard Shultz, personally demonstrated his commitment to this development of the team by providing guidance at the outset of the forum. He also attended and participated in various parts of the workshop over the 3 days. As was his custom, he spoke of the company heritage and the passion for the people and the product of Starbucks. Importantly, at the end of the 3 days, each participant was asked to speak personally of the connection to each other and the mission of Starbucks and how to elevate their leadership. It is world-class leadership commitment and development and it was unforgettable in my career journey. This is genuinely taking responsibility in heart, mind and soul.

This chapter is devoted to techniques and experiences that relate to successfully recruiting, selecting, hiring, training and developing a highly effective team of people. Starting with the best team and creating a learning organization whether big or small is the engine that drives success. It comes from the Heart!

Taking Responsibility for Leading People

Key Takeaways:
- ✓ *Strategy:* Senior Leaders should have expert skills in both Managing and Leading.
- ✓ *Basic:* Leading and Managing require different skill sets.
- ✓ *Execution:* Managing requires strong technical knowledge and orientation to detail – implement training that creates competence in technical skills.
- ✓ *Execution:* Leading requires authentic concern for people and a desire to help others – implement programs and workshops that develop leaders.

Search for the Best People

No matter what the business or organization, finding good people is a pivotal piece that sustains, as well as elevates, the work product. The search for these people should not just be to fill holes left by others that depart. A good and thoughtful leader is always looking for hard-working, talented people in advance of need or crisis. It makes sense, in advance of a potential turnover, to invest in avoiding holes or a crisis situation. Also, often there are people in position that are struggling in the organization, and planning for their replacement is critical. Staff shortages or crisis can cause the most harm to the customer, team morale, and business results than any other challenge faced by a leader. Only having the wrong people in place can be more pressing.

Searching for a leader is not yet recruiting. This daily quest is about being strategic, resourceful and passionate about sizing up people that are in the daily routine for a possible fit. Other businesses, community functions, a colleague from the past, suppliers, associates of trusted friends and basically anywhere your life takes you, provide opportunities to search. Smart and successful leaders are always searching for the next great hire.

My wife Kathy and I started planning in early 2013 to open our Red Mango yogurt, smoothie and juice bar. Kathy is an outstanding mother, but she was not part of the daily business grind I was involved in other than the stories I brought home. She had more important experience than me in our household by far, but leading and managing business activities would all be new to her. We both thought our partnership in this enterprise would be as successful and productive as it ultimately was, but building blocks were needed.

I was still in touch with a colleague, actually my training manager when I joined Starbucks. Her name is Beth Fink. I admired her extreme attention to detail and strong commitment and the understanding of what it takes to teach people repeatable behaviors and routines, operations basics. Beth is also an individual of high ethics, a high character person. It occurred to me that since I would be continuing to work in my corporate leadership role at Smile Brands, we would need a leader like Beth to partner with Kathy and get the store off the ground effectively.

I took a shot, knowing Beth was not working at the time but had been employed by a competing yogurt purveyor in Southern California. I also knew the compensation we could afford would be less than what she was qualified to receive. Nonetheless, Beth took the call and she was excited to help us get the store off the ground and teach Kathy the ropes the right way. This was a very important day in our nearly 5-year history of owning that store.

Beth worked with us for 18 months and led the recruitment effort to hire the initial staff, manage the details to get the store open, market the store to grow sales rapidly, and teach and coach Kathy from experience over a long Starbucks career. Her extensive training background enabled her, alongside Kathy, to lead the process of group interviewing, hiring and training the initial staff. This work embedded standards of operation in our store that sustained for the entire time we owned the store. She coached Kathy on interviewing techniques and basics that led to successful hiring. Everything that Beth brought us in that first 18-months helped develop Kathy into an outstanding store operator.

Strategically searching for a great fit in any organization and nurturing that commitment has the unparalleled potential of any other decisions and actions a leader takes.

Taking Responsibility to Search for the Best People

Key Takeaways:
- ✓ *Strategy:* Selecting the right people is imperative to success.
- ✓ *Execution:* Drive a constant search for people as part of the daily routine.
- ✓ *Execution:* Priority focus to recruit and search for great fits for the team.
- ✓ *Execution:* "Take a shot" with great people to recruit and elevate rapidly.

Encourage, Influence and Recruit the Best People

There are rare times that you see a "blue chip" leader and become familiar with their talents and character. "Blue Chip" is a metaphor coming from the game of Poker referencing the most valuable chips as part of the game. With people, these are the most valuable and fit high expectations to elevate the performance of the organization as a near certainty of success. Having them on your team enhances the performance of others and brings innovation and fresh approaches to elevate. In addition to this, they understand what it means to be a team player. When this happens, a hiring leader must take all reasonable steps to get this person on the team.

At 7-Eleven and Starbucks, we often used the process of group interviews, as part of succession planning, for hiring or promoting internal & external senior level positions. Many candidates came with recommendations from current managers or other employees. There would be 3-5 interviewers brought together, including direct reports and senior human resources staff. This approach calibrated expectations for what we wanted and needed in individuals we were considering for key leadership roles. The team learned from each other and drilled company *success profiles* (standards of behaviors related to successful leaders) for the roles.

Group interviews in the operating regions were day-long events, minimum once per quarter, where we would meet several candidates for 60-90 minutes each. There may be specific markets in which we had focus, but all of the interviewers actively participated and questioned the candidates to help evaluate skill sets and leadership competencies in detail. Copious notes were taken in each session to provide valid and tangible discussion after interviews were completed.

At the end of the day of group interviews, the team would meet for 60 to 90 minutes afterwards to discuss our individual assessment of each candidate as potential hires or potential promotes. Using tools, such as the *success profiles* and answers or impressions from the interviews, we would come up with our next steps. We would make hiring decisions on the best candidates. The other candidates would be given feedback on development needed for future consideration.

Giving feedback, most especially to candidates that are not being selected, is essential. This may be uncomfortable, but it is the responsibility of the leader to help the candidate understand what they can do to improve and develop skills or experience to be selected for future opportunities. It is also being considerate and professional. One or two specific areas of opportunity with suggested effort in their current job will help the candidate and perhaps motivate them to improve in readiness. In many cases, it is a close call and the skill and experience areas are sound. It would be important to communicate that and highlight the specific strengths. In my experience, candidates receiving this feedback are appreciative. If not, it is one more indicator the right decision is being made on the candidate that is selected.

This practice or "basic" of team interviews is instrumental in developing high standards of expectations and detailed analysis for the most important decision a leader makes– selecting key leaders. The time spent is significant, but it is rich in giving the candidate and the organization the best chance at success. Even with internal candidates, where a track record of performance is more readily known, the process provides a unique insight into strengths and opportunities. Leveraging the brain power of the leader team improves the quality of the decisions.

At 7-Eleven, Starbucks and Smile Brands, we had high-performing sustainable regional teams of leaders with excellent retention. A vast majority of each one of the individuals on those teams has either progressed in their careers at the current company or moved on to senior leader roles with other companies. There are several VP's, a few senior or executive VP's and two COO's to date. It is a great source of pride to see the legacy of great people gaining much from their work, and it started with the ever-important decision to select them as a next-level leader.

Taking Responsibility to Encourage, Influence and Recruit the Best People

Key Takeaways:
- ✓ *Strategy:* Implement succession planning to hire and promote high potential leaders for all key positions.
- ✓ *Execution:* Use a team process to interview and consider the top pool of candidates.
- ✓ *Execution:* Use a debrief meeting to get feedback from interviewers.
- ✓ *Execution:* Leverage the interview team to be responsible (ensure "buy in") for the selection decision.

Teach, Train and Develop with a Heart

Developing leaders and succession planning is a responsibility that is more important to sustained success than any other investment expended in an organization. It requires a sincere belief in and commitment to the principle that people are the most important resource in any business or organization. A longer-term outlook with incremental milestones and goals tailored to the individual, a plan, should be the focus of the leader from the day the team member enters the organization, until they exit. When the leader owns the responsibility in a genuine way (not just delegated) the potential for success is maximized in measurable results and return on invested time and money. This all means that every leader in the organization is grounded in a "culture" of people development.

A successful leader is a solid teacher and is always looking for ways to broaden knowledge of the product, process and best practices. Constantly improving and reducing inefficiencies and redundancies come from this approach. Teaching is connecting the dots and being observant and curious enough to know the good and the bad and communicating generously, many times informally. I often consider how I've borrowed from the best teachers I've encountered in order to connect with individual people effectively. Everybody can list the great teachers they have had in school, college, companies and organizations, communities, and in each family.

At 7-Eleven, I had the great fortune to work with and for some outstanding teachers over 22 years in 14 different positions. When asked about my educational background, I sometimes joke that I have an MBA in convenient stores. It is practical knowledge that has been invaluable to every other experience inside and outside of business. Being an invested and interested learner in any position enables richness from leaders who usually do not realize what great teachers they are. It is a successful behavior to be an attentive learner and pay it forward in order to become a great teacher.

While a teacher generally is characterized by the ability to connect with the individual personally, the trainer should be for more focused on curriculum, standards, details and technical skill development. Trainers, to be effective, must have order and discipline with check-ins to assess that the trainee is successfully understanding and executing the skills being developed. In other words, trainers should be masters at the practical application of the skill and their detailed observation of execution is the skill assessment.

In 1982, as the Zone Training Manager in San Jose, CA for 7-Eleven, I built experience in training others. Training was always something I enjoyed, and I was thrilled to have the responsibility to train new franchisees and management people in the 100 plus store Zone. The program responsibilities included 2-weeks of in-store training for each new franchisee or management team member that they were required to successfully complete. This was comprised of practical training related to ordering, stocking goods, making schedules, daily reports, banking, serving customers, cleaning duties and all key aspects of store operations.

I learned the huge importance of helping others prepare for success in operating an annual million-dollar business, by leading training of new franchisees. This franchising experience was their livelihood for their life and family. I felt the weight of the responsibility in heart, mind and soul, to be thorough and disciplined to ensure that they were ready to take on the business. One 7-Eleven store had 2500 items and 1000 daily tasks, much of which are delegated. Being just the warm teacher of trainees that were "under my wing"' would not meet the mark.

Great trainers are more than teachers. 7-Eleven enabled me to learn *command* in leadership by allowing me to see the business from the place that made the company successful in helping franchisees succeed. I spent 20 more years with 7-Eleven, but this experience helped me understand the critical impact training has on any enterprise. When does the teaching and training end? Simple: it never ends.

Every successful organization is a learning organization. When the leader of a company has all the answers, look for stormy days ahead. Every individual in any organization requires daily development of leadership and skill. People development is about commitment that balances structured and informal coaching and instruction. 7-Eleven, Starbucks and Smile Brands all had key leaders that showed that commitment to professional development. It was instrumental to success within each company.

Taking Responsibility to Teach, Train and Develop with a Heart

Key Takeaways:
- ✓ *Strategy:* High priority commitment to leadership development.
- ✓ *Basic:* Reinforce a culture of people development as a leader responsibility.
- ✓ *Execution:* Create a culture of leader-led teaching that is informal and personal.
- ✓ *Execution:* Develop skills training that is disciplined, structured and repetitive.

Now, Discover Your Strengths

At Starbucks, in 2003, there was the beginning of a standard practice to initiate team meetings and workshops in regions & markets that began with a "strength finder analysis" from the book by Marcus Buckingham and David Clifton. With the book, each participant took an online survey that established their 5 "signature themes" of strengths they possess out of a possible 34. The "strengths" enable each participant to understand areas in their leadership style that are natural ways to leverage positive outcomes.

In team development, this exercise helps facilitate a clear method to understand and leverage the personalities on the team. For a leader, it pinpoints areas where the team is well-balanced or maybe has opportunities to strategically add people with strengths currently unavailable. Also, the discussion piece of the workshop has each participant seeing the signature themes of colleagues that illustrate the mix of strengths on the team. It's fun to share as a group exercise and it helps the team build relationships and highlight improved ways to work together for success.

Starting in 2003 and throughout the balance of my corporate leadership career, until 2016, I used *Now, Discover Your Strength* workshops numerous times with different and changing teams. I found this an excellent way to build relationships and, subsequently teams, to more empirically understand the group and individual development. By the way, maybe not surprisingly, my number one strength from this exercise… *responsibility*.

Taking Responsibility to implement Now, Discover Your Strengths

Key Takeaways:
- ✓ *Basic: Now, Discover Your Strengths* survey brings insights to develop a team sensibly.
- ✓ *Execution:* Schedule preparation and workshops using data from StrengthFinders assessment tool.
- ✓ *Execution:* Leader led workshop to review StrengthFinders insights for fun, engagement and in planning for team productivity.

<u>**Place Talent with an Eye on Team Fit**</u>

Team productivity translates into measurable results.

The skill on the team blended with the motivation and willingness at strong levels nets the best possible opportunity for success. Productivity is largely about the leader and key decisions made to empower team members and mobilizing them with work plans (of which they are a part). Performance and productivity also come from a competitive spirit and the constant drive to improve the work product. All of this requires skilled and motivated people that communicate effectively with each other.

Vision in leadership relates to the ability of the leader to see into the future and around corners. This skill is imperative in setting up an organization for success. Not every leader possesses this ability. Leaders with vision understand obstacles before they occur. With this, they surround themselves with team members that have the capability to confront and address negative influences. Leaders with vision also pick team members who have creative and innovative approaches to "hit the gas," drive performance and propel growth.

The New England Patriots have mastered the skill of placing talent and raising the bar more than any NFL Team in modern times. The team has 6 Super Bowl victories since 2001 under Coach Bill Belichick. Tom Brady was not a standout player in college and barely started 1 year at Michigan. He is now arguably the finest NFL quarterback in history. With other positions, New England constantly evolve and make head-scratching changes year-in and year-out on veteran football players. Other than Brady, it would be difficult to point to many players in the last 15 or so years that are so valuable that the team doesn't succeed without them. All of this is due to vision and excellent leadership related to finding players that fit.

Making decisions on team fit starts with talent of each individual. Though this may not mean the top or most talented, any selection decision should be highly regarded individuals with a combination of top skills, work ethic and track record. Also, personality is a component that I view as an intangible. It is not a primary piece but is clearly important, especially at the early stages of joining the team. With this, using objective facts supported by others around the leader, helps make a "team fit" decision successful. The key question: Will this individual hit the ground running and make the team better in month 1? Also, can the leader "squint" and see them as highly productive and successful in the months and years down the road?

Down the road is about raising the bar. Bill Belichick would have been fired years ago if he did not set a "Patriot" standard that won the team 6 Super Bowls. At Starbucks, the stock price and record-setting growth over decades comes from standards set long ago through constant improvement. 7-Eleven invented the convenient store business model 75 years ago, evolved through rough waters, remade the process and have flourished by raising the bar successfully. Smile Brands has bounced back by finding itself in varying approaches to restart the success it previously enjoyed. Each of these examples relate to successful organizations I know well and organizations that have had the vision to maneuver rough waters and leverage talented and motivated people to raise the bar effectively. This is taking responsibility in heart, mind and soul.

When I joined Smile Brands in 2009, my new team looked to be a motivated group with strong work ethic. The team also had a deep knowledge of dental services that I lacked in almost every way with the exception of being a dental patient. When I met with the CEO prior to my hire, I was impressed with his energy and vision. He was interested in bringing in leaders to help move the organization to the next level. I was at Starbucks and the idea of helping a small company create excellent patient experiences energized me. It was a monumental change for me, but the idea of building a team in healthcare, a space missing in my background, was very exciting.

The move proved rewarding, but it was also frustrating, humbling and extremely challenging. It taxed every leadership competency I possessed but enabled significant personal growth. I would like to say that the experience was everything I intended when I joined Smile Brands in 2009, but that would not be true.

The company purchase by a new investor group in late 2010 proved to be unsuccessful. Serious revenue and EBITDA (earnings before interest, taxes, depreciation and amortization) declines resulted from questionable decisions related to aggressively adding new offices, along with other market related headwinds. This ultimately led to the departure of the CEO Steve Bilt in late 2013.

A new CEO was appointed by the investors. Many other senior leadership changes immediately followed. Our operating routine dramatically changed with a top down daily review of office dentist and hygienist production metrics. We transformed from a patient and dentist-centric culture to a metrics-driven culture. My team was being micro-managed by headquarters management and that was becoming difficult for me to buffer. I could no longer align myself with the direction. I took responsibility for my team in heart, mind and soul. This ultimately caused me to push back, give direct feedback to the CEO and resign citing the intolerable approach being taken by his lieutenants.

The salient point here relates to "fit." Others may have gelled perfectly with this approach to drive the revenue and improve the value of the business for the sale of the company at direction of private investors.

That was not my skill set, career direction or values after nearly 7 years of leading in a much different way to help Smile Brands develop through patient facing initiative.

I am grateful to Dan Wechsler, the then CEO, for treating my resignation with understanding and respect. There was much appreciated recognition and celebration at the Annual Leadership Conference in January 2016 when I departed. That was an act of class. I believe Dan was under pressure to show short term results demanded by the investors to effectively divest Smile Brands which prompted survival methods his senior team was employing. This action I took to resign was best to serve Smile Brands and myself at that time. I self-selected in this decision based on "fit" to the organization.

With that background, I will always remember the incredible team I led, many for the whole time I was part of Smile Brands. In particular, Claudia Perez comes to mind as a leader that excelled with strong work ethic and a strong desire to succeed. Claudia started with Smile Brands in the 1990's as a dental assistant and worked her way through many roles.

Claudia was attending college at night to finish her degree successfully, while working more than full-time and being an outstanding mom to 4 young children. I watched in amazement as this exceptional woman juggled all the many demanding leadership responsibilities of her job with the care of her wonderful family, while improving herself with academic accomplishment.

Claudia energetically helped her colleagues and managers by translating leadership growth concepts like Situational Leadership and Servant Leadership. This work was instrumental to the culture change we led- she is a catalyst of transformation. Claudia has a remarkable story of taking responsibility in heart, mind and soul. A perfect "fit" and an extremely valuable "Blue Chip" leader on my team.

Throughout my tenure at Smile Brands, we interviewed dozens of potential leaders for key leadership positions. The primary objective of finding the correct "fit" to change the culture was difficult. The Dental sector has longtime leaders that generally move from one company to the next- many have worked for 3 or 4 different organizations with similar leadership challenges. Most of these leaders had exceptional knowledge of dentistry, billing, regulatory issues and compliance with sub-par customer (patient) service skill sets.

We brought in former retail and food service professionals as a way to improve the culture of service at Smile Brands. Tom Penn and Liam Kelly from Starbucks are examples of excellent people leaders we infused into our team successfully. They both excelled as leaders during my time at Starbucks where I worked with them previously. At the same time, the cultural shift at Smile Brands was extremely tough mainly due to the time it takes to learn important aspects of the dental sector or healthcare in general. It took a lot of effort and commitment for Liam, Tom and me to make the transition together. Colleagues like Claudia Perez and Lorilee Schmidt, longtime successful dental sector leaders, were very helpful.

An update after my departure is that the original CEO Steve Bilt, engineered a repurchase of the company to return to Smile Brands in late 2016. From the outside, it looks like the company is returning to the people culture and a growing company in the dental service organization arena. It is great to see Steve and his team return to the values that provided the great foundation of Smile Brands that attracted me to join. And, great news! Over a year ago, Claudia Perez was promoted to Vice President.

Taking Responsibility to Place Talent with an Eye on Team Fit

Key Takeaways:
- ✓ *Strategy:* Ensure culture is maintained and elevated by focus on team "fit" of new hires and promoted leaders.
- ✓ *Basic:* Talent, work ethic and track record are components of success.

✓ *Execution:* Select team members that have ability to be productive day one.
✓ *Execution:* "Fit" should be part of a plan to meet the needs of the leader and the team.

Reward the Best Performers using Objective Facts

Productive people are the "difference makers" in any business or organization. Those people deserve the most support, recognition, rewards and compensation from their leaders. Colin Powell said this in his Leadership Primer: "Trying to get everyone to like you is a sign of mediocrity: you'll avoid the tough decisions, you'll avoid confronting the people who need to be confronted, and you'll avoid offering differential rewards based on differential performance because some people might get upset." I believe in the wisdom of General Powell's Leadership Principles and to this assertion completely.

People usually learn more from one another than from their boss or leader. Leaders that strive to perform at a high level observe and learn from colleagues that are examples of taking responsibility for action and results. Welcoming and informally leading colleagues brings a culture of team development. Every leader must have people on their team with an inclination to help others to succeed, and that inspires others to do the same. This atmosphere also promotes a healthy competition where everyone learns and wants to win individually *and* collectively.

Obviously, results matter in order to be successful. If a leader is willing to regularly outline, in a public way, the measurable and objective results of their people, especially the top performers, it will lead to a culture of high performance. Without this leadership recognition complacency and declining productivity can result. It also invites lack of spirit & teamwork which is a death knell for any organization and a failure of leadership. Leaders are responsible in heart, mind and soul to motivate their teams and spotlight the great work, performance and results of their people.

In a business environment, it is important to have very frequent and visible review of sales and profit reporting by business unit (store, department, district, region etc.). Daily, weekly and monthly disciplined review of results, led by the business unit leader, keeps the culture of accountability alive and constant. For example, daily reporting should be on e-mail with a standard reporting process like flash sales. Weekly process should connect the team via team call with each business unit leader briefly updating overall results for the week.

Periodic (monthly, quarterly) in-person team meetings with review of results by each unit leader and discussion of challenges and successes, serve the team well. Disciplined communication processes around measurable results solidify the notion of "why we are here" with any team or organization. It also enables the leader and the team to elevate the top performers as role models and provides frequent opportunity for reward and recognition. Associated with this forum is discussion around action plans to drive results and address opportunities and problem areas.

In a period of challenging or poor performance, which is inevitable, leaders will feel the pressure in experiencing negative trends. Obviously, frequent review of measurable results during tough periods can bring the spirits of the team downward. It is the responsibility of the leader to smooth the process. This will help the team and individuals remain confident and focused on action to regain positive momentum. Action plans must be honed and realistic about the priorities that yield wins in taking responsibility.

While budget requirements exist, the actions must be rich in helping the team and the individuals see that their work is on track and leading to budget goal or expectation. Setting direction and keeping to the standard of achieving goals while showing an active support of the team members is imperative. There is a delicate balance of how the unit leader approaches sub-par performance, but regular communication and assessment of the situation will promote an upward reversal of poor trends.

Error to the side of "pats on the back" and adding positive energy to team members that show strong performance and leadership in work and key initiatives. In public, it is important to reinforce the great work of team members by recognition and listing the big wins. In some cases, recognizing high performers in front of their peers with rewards or gifts is indicated and appropriate. They walk away with a lasting memory and knowing they are making a difference. People gain confidence from this and it adds to the culture of winning.

With prolonged poor performance, individual action plans and, in some cases, corrective measures should be considered. Team members need help at times to turn negative trends around. The plan to correct serious performance problems must be addressed with urgency. Done in private, a leader can ensure that the individual is not being embarrassed in front of peers but still receives a firm message that they are responsible their results. Coaching action plans and getting acknowledgement from individuals struggling with measurable results is the responsibility of the leader. Good communication and *calibration* of standards gives a much better chance at success in these cases.

If there is a lack of accountability, or failure to accept responsibility for poor performance, the unit leader should initiate a rich and direct conversation with the team member. Words like "unacceptable" and "intolerable" related to the performance and results will ensure clarity and seriousness. Also, emphasizing that the unit leader is taking responsibility to help the team member address and fix their performance positively clarifies the mission. This honest communication will likely lead to ownership of the work by the team member. If not, it will indicate a more serious problem.

It is difficult to formally counsel subordinates with poor results and/or performance, but it is overwhelmingly essential. Doing this with a one or two-page maximum outline is the best approach. Start with enumeration of the measurable results below budget or standard. State that the results are unacceptable and must be improved. List any behaviors or performance areas that contribute to the below expectation results. Ask for a written action plan by a specific date to take responsibility and address the results. And, finish this written document with a statement that the expectation is that the results and performance must be corrected with specific timeframes and check-ins ("further disciplinary action up to and including termination" is something I strongly recommend). Also, include human resources professionals in the process of counseling as is standard in most organizations. This is "business" and "not personal" and I generally stated that point at least once in such counseling.

Objective facts must be the measurement of the performance of the team, leader and the individual team members. Quantitative information is the report card for leaders and teams in business or professional organizations. The facts should be used primarily to create *differential* rewards for strongest performance in public settings or team meetings and forums. It is the key to sustained winning and consistent success.

Taking Responsibility to Reward the Best Performers using Objective Facts:

Key Takeaways:
- ✓ *Strategy:* Recognize and reward leaders and team members that achieve top performance and results.
- ✓ *Execution:* Disciplined review of daily, weekly & monthly results and performance.
- ✓ *Execution:* Focus on wins and healthy competition as a culture.
- ✓ *Execution:* Privately correct poor results individually.
- ✓ *Execution:* Formally counsel in writing when sub-standard results/performance continue.

Create Healthy Competition with Recognition

In building teams, bias toward competitive people that enjoy setting records and driving performance numbers and results is invaluable. Being competitive in most business situations means being creative, resourceful and optimistic. These are intangible characteristics of high performers and I am fortunate to have been associated with a very large number of these individuals over my career. To have these people on any team can easily make the difference in achievement of goals necessary with the business unit or organization.

I must emphasize that "healthy competition" means productive, energetic and fun discourse on the team related to results. There might be organized incentives and contests that rank performers or just daily nudging on important initiatives. It is pretty clear people enjoy well-spirited competition. When properly leveraged, it can be a huge difference-maker in results. The unit leader must have a healthy and unifying tone that inspires the team to reach higher. Simply, when one individual on the team wins, the team wins and the spirit of this breeds success and pride.

Taking Responsibility to Create Healthy Competition with Recognition:

Key Takeaways:
- ✓ *Strategy:* Healthy competition often makes the difference in achieving goals.
- ✓ *Basic:* Leader sets the tone in unifying a competitive team.
- ✓ *Execution:* Create and communicate fun contests and challenges related to sales or profit performance by unit, district and region.

Retain the Best People – Know Them and Care about Them

The biggest secret to sustaining and driving the performance of a business unit or organization is retention. It keeps the best people on the team. Retaining the best people gives the organization the highest chance of success. Spending inordinate amounts of time, money and brainpower on refilling the pipeline with talent and developing that talent is necessary but it cannot become a way of life. Good turnover is when a sub-par or average performer exits voluntarily or involuntarily. Poor turnover is everything else. A great, experienced and high-performing team member leaving for another organization is disastrous. This should not surprise a leader if they truly know and care about their people.

Retaining the best people is a prime responsibility of the unit leader. A sense of belonging and value related to each member of the team emanates from the unit leader and how they treat each individual. Communication as a group and individually must demonstrate a genuine concern for career development, aspirations, problem solving, compensation, work/life balance and appreciation for good work. The connection each individual has to the leader and the team predicts job satisfaction for the short term and long term. Not surprisingly, based on research by countless experts, people leave people (bosses)– not just organizations, companies or business units.

A leader cannot fake the genuine concern and consideration they have for their people. Individuals know when a leader is disconnected, disengaged, lacking empathy or self-centered. "Tough but fair" is great, but tough and any of these 4 negative characteristics previously listed is begging for an exodus, especially by the best people. Successful leaders come in many styles and forms but the best leaders, with consistently strong performance, love their people and their people know it. Trust is built by the "real deal" in an organization where open and honest communication exists with a human touch, not unlike a family.

7-Eleven, Starbucks and Smile Brands were all very different organizations with very different cultures. However, my greatest feeling now is the remarkable connections that still remain from people that worked with me and those who I was able to serve as their leader or subordinate.

One of my closest friends in life, Miguel Foegal, is someone I followed in 3 positions after promotions at 7-Eleven in the early 1980's. He mentored me on how to lead and bring a team together. Miguel visited stores unannounced ("lone wolf tours") as a daily routine to assess the service franchisees received from his staff. He would help out with daily tasks and assist with such problems as maintenance of equipment. He served his team and was not afraid of showing he cared by working alongside and coaching his team of people. This is a practice I followed in every position throughout my career.

Miguel's grasp of the convenience business was unbelievable, but his charisma and style were unique. He was firm in his direction but each one of his valued field consultants and franchisees knew he had their back. He made it clear and he taught me how important human connection is to be successful in leadership. We live in different states now, but hardly a day goes by without a text exchange on current events or not surprisingly, chatting about people we love, like our grandkids. I appreciate the imprint Miguel left on me as a person and as a leader.

At Starbucks, there were a number of role model leaders I was able to see in action. The leader that stands out the most to me is Mark Lindstrom, my leader and boss for 3 years. Mark showed me the path to be not only a productive executive, but he modeled the way to bring a large billion-dollar sales unit together with "one team and one purpose." He remains extremely well-regarded by store managers, district managers and regional directors in the largest division in Starbucks at the time. He personally called select store managers daily with sincere concern for them and their teams – there were 1400 stores in his Division at the time. Many times, it was to thank a store manager for a good sales month or a special action in helping an employee or for superior customer service.

Mark's personal touch is something I took away and practiced in my own leadership. Mark genuinely loved and cared about his team and showed it. Much like his personal calls, his genuine personal notes of congratulations to store people were "from the heart" and related to the wins they were accomplishing. Mark made a very big job smaller and real. Mark taught me unforgettable lessons on nurturing the important relationships you have with the team you lead. He is an outstanding leader and even a better person.

Miguel and Mark kept great teams together with longevity. Those teams delivered results regardless of poor economies or company issues that weren't always positive. To this day, loyalty to these two men is immense for people that had the privilege to work with them, like myself. The recipe for success with retention is centered around the approach these leaders demonstrated daily with their teams of people. They are role models for leading people from the "heart," which is a fundamental of success that cannot be under estimated. Miguel and Mark took responsibility for their teams over decades in heart, mind and soul.

**Taking Responsibility to Retain the Best People –
Know Them and Care about Them:**

Key Takeaways:
- ✓ *Strategy:* Ensure retention of high performing people.
- ✓ *Execution:* Get to know each individual on the team – building relationships part of the culture.
- ✓ *Execution:* Implement a robust recognition program for top performance.
- ✓ *Execution:* Informally demonstrate genuine and sincere care for individuals, especially high performers on the team.

Chapter Three

<u>Managing the Core Business (Mind)</u>

Effective leadership in any organization requires form, order, methods and functions that have a history of success with proven outcomes. There are longstanding disciplines that are readily shared in business and other organizations that enable people to measure results daily, weekly and monthly. These disciplines gauge learning and help make decision-making less risky and have the best potential for success. This is important for any leader to use the power of rational, objective thought and help the team succeed.

Many argue that great leaders have excellent instincts, intuition or "gut feel." That is probably true but anything from the "gut" is proven over a long time with a track record of performance. Error to the side of facts when making decisions. It is foolhardy to believe that "winging it" or "shooting from the hip" is wise with key decisions. Importantly, every decision that risks financial success or another key measure, is the responsibility of the unit leader. Thinking these decisions through with enough factual data and expert analysis is better than just having a good feeling that may or may not be grounded in solid experiences.

At 7-Eleven in the mid to late 1980's, we began implementing the retail practice and business process called *Tanpin Kanri*. The company went through significant financial challenges in the United States after a tremendous run of success over several decades– in particular the 1960's, 70's and into the 80's. By 1985, the financial pressure coming from new and improved convenience competition became so severe it required widespread downsizing of leadership positions and lower margins. Overuse of price promotion on beer, wine and cigarettes shrunk the margins.

7-Eleven's inability to evolve ultimately led to a leveraged buyout of the company by the 7-Eleven Japan licensee with an orderly bankruptcy to accomplish the transaction. Toward the end of the 1980's the partner licensee of the parent company became the new private owner of the entire 7-Eleven store chain. The introduction of *Tanpin Kanri* or the new business process was not far behind the purchase.

Tanpin Kanri is a retail practice that essentially means item-by-item management. It is designed to put order and discipline with factual analysis surrounding adding and deleting items, top seller product management, planograms or merchandising and all of the basics related to understanding trends of sales by item and category. *Tanpin Kanri* happens at the headquarters level, the regional level and most importantly at the store level. The process had documented success at 7-Eleven Japan for over a decade. The 2011 Harvard Business Review article *"Tanpin Kanri*: Retail Practice at Seven-Eleven Japan" details the history.

Prior to the implementation of this enterprise-saving business approach, 7-Eleven in the United States was mired in a spiral of decline due to betting on price promotions that yielded single-digit margins on the major core commodity products in each store. The business was managed globally in offices far away from the customer. Feedback from franchisees or store operators was either given little credence or was outright rejected. The company people made all of the critical decisions on how to take product to the stores and vendors were 'in charge' of price and placement decisions effectively delegated to them by company merchandising personnel.

In this chapter, I will take you through the remake of 7-Eleven Incorporated (formerly Southland Corporation) that I am proud to say I was a part of in the 1990's. My experience, along with thousands of other people working with 7-Eleven at the time, embraced the *Tanpin Kanri* retail practice with tremendous teamwork. The work led to a business turnaround that taught us all rich lessons.

Tanpin Kanri as a Basic

There is an adage in managing the retail business, "retail is detail." At 7-Eleven there was tremendous success and value created over decades prior to the 1980's. The successful convenience business concept created in the late 1920's by Joe C Thompson & family with 7-Eleven in Dallas, Texas (formerly "Totem" until 1947). The growth of the convenience store concept originated from an ice dock that evolved with grocery items added including bread, milk, eggs and other customer daily needs to create a business catering to customers in a time pressured need state.

By the 1960's, the growth of the product mix and categories soared, and complexity and challenges followed. The complexities were tackled at that time by franchising stores to independent operators that lived in the neighborhoods and understood the customers. It was a stroke of genius that propelled the chain to exponential growth and success that carried for nearly two decades from the mid-1960's until the mid-1980's. Proprietary (exclusively 7-Eleven) categories like Slurpee, coffee and fountain soft drinks to complement the other core commodity categories in each store created differentiation or a barrier to entry for competition.

However, with over 2000 items carried in each average 7-Eleven store in 1985, compounded by a disjointed and ineffective communication process between headquarters trailing to individual stores was causing the chain to fail. New and improved competitors were fighting for their piece of market share with better information systems, very similar product offerings and hungrier people. The "retail is detail" notion was disappearing from the 7-Eleven culture. Headquarters product management and direction was failing due to a "we have always overcome" mindset.

During this period, poor expense control, bad financial decisions and poor product cost management took place at every level of the bloated, complacent organization. Sales growth, once robust, was no longer happening and price promotion on core business categories yielded steeply declining margins. In some cases, such as cigarettes and beer, margins were nearly zero. The chain was headed to bankruptcy.

After the needed leveraged buyout to save the 7-Eleven North American business, Seven-Eleven Japan almost immediately began the long journey of implementing *Tanpin Kanri*. It was a culture changing effort that organically chased out senior leaders that couldn't or wouldn't be a part of a comprehensive change in the management process of the 7-Eleven business. The mantra of *Tanpin Kanri,* or "TK" as we all called it, was "deny the status quo" and implement the "retailer initiative" business concept. This meant every leader and team member should prepare for major change in the work they do or look elsewhere for employment. We were in a fight for survival and SEJ was providing a clear culture change message. TK was "simple" but it was not "easy."

Most franchisees were nervous, but many understood that monumental change was necessary to succeed going forward. Franchisees represented 65% of the 7-Eleven business nationally at that time. It was imperative to get them, as well as the very jittery corporate leaders like myself, acclimated to the change in business strategy and approach. The belief in the tenets of TK was bolstered by a very comprehensive teaching process developed and executed by the most senior management at 7-Eleven– from Clark Matthews the CEO to the store manager ("Clerk to Clark").

Every leader was mobilized to Field offices and individual stores to execute week-long workshops for Field Leaders to immerse in TK – the discipline of managing the business for all stores in North America. All of this work included paper and pen – a very manual process – to retrain the mindset of the store ordering and operations. I would compare it to learning math without a calculator, which was very labor intensive but rich in outcome.

The beginning of the conversation related to TK with all of the stores and stakeholders was "ordering is the number one job" of each 7-Eleven store. We were tasked with practicing manual ordering of each individual item using a large binder of order sheets divided by categories and by suppliers. With this, we used a 4-step thought process of the following:

1) **Observation:** this is the *current situation analysis* that included trends related to seasonal weather, events in the area, holidays, competitive considerations and the actual sales of the item over the past 4 weeks.
2) **Hypothesis:** this part of the process has the order writer question how many more items could be sold by making merchandising display changes (for example adding facings of product) or making changes by reducing slow moving items that this item may substitute effectively.
3) **Execution:** taking action or implementing the changes in the hypothesis and collecting sales data.
4) **Review:** Analyzing the sales data on the item resulting from the changes executed.

This 4-step process is a concise replica of the scientific method used across most fields of study. 7-Eleven used this to add new high potential items and delete slow sellers in a discipline called "narrowing" the product assortment. No longer were the order writers "winging it." This had a significant and nearly immediate impact on reducing out of stocks or missed opportunities and making room for new "high potential" items customers would be looking to buy. There was a strong focus on "never, ever running out of top selling items" which is fundamental with a convenience retailing point of view.

Taking Responsibility to implement *Tanpin Kanri* as a Basic

Key Takeaways:
- ✓ *Strategy: Tanpin Kanri* (TK) the process with product focus item by item.
- ✓ *Strategy:* Ordering "number one job" of each store
- ✓ *Basic:* "Retail is Detail."
- ✓ *Execution:* System-wide "Clerk to Clark" culture change workshops.
- ✓ *Execution:* "Never, ever run out" of top selling items.
- ✓ *Execution:* Add high potential items customers want to buy.
- ✓ *Execution:* Use data to delete slow sellers.

Longevity of 7-Eleven Bolstered by *Tanpin Kanri*:

7-Eleven in North America has thrived nearly 30 years after a bankruptcy and transformation by leaning on the business process of *Tanpin Kanri* (TK). As an operations and merchandising field and headquarters leader, during and after the bankruptcy, I witnessed relentless, determined and steadily successful outcomes. This came from passionate focus on the basics of TK. It was "simple" but not "easy" to use the words of senior leaders in prodding the hard work that was taking place every day. A large behemoth of a company with a wonderful heritage was slowly and patiently being resurrected.

In my leadership career at 7-Eleven, Starbucks and

Smile Brands I often borrowed what I learned from the wisdom of Seven Eleven Japan senior leaders. TK is about "Living in the Basics." Some companies like Budweiser describe this as KISS method or "keep it simple stupid" which is all about repeatable routine. My purpose was rooted in the notion that if you relentlessly live in the basics of item by item management, you will never have to go "back to the basics," a phrase that admits taking one's "eye off the ball." When I heard store managers and field leaders tell me they were going "back to the basics" I became very concerned about the business process that was expected under their leadership.

Culturally, in any organization, having a repeatable routine led and owned by the store manager enables consistency of ordering, customer service, product standards and training of the staff that leads to success. Again, this is simple but not easy, and fundamental in a multi-unit operations organization.

In the 12-years I worked at 7-Eleven *after* the bankruptcy and through the transformation, the TK business process and passionate execution of it, forever changed my approach to leadership. Though not formal, this yielded a "Master's" in convenience store retailing with ordering as the number one job of the store. Never, ever running out of top selling items and introducing new high potential items brought a dynamic focus on a renewed product mix that favored items customers wanted to buy.

Though I left 7-Eleven in 2002, the growth of the business has continued to prosper. The reason: 7-Eleven has a built-in, sustainable business process that enables stores not to miss the front end of a product life cycle and evolve and adapt using the TK process not creating new processes. On the flip side, when the store sees a product on the downside of a product life cycle, the product can be replaced in the assortment.

As part of the TK implementation, we also leveraged a term called "retailer initiative." Simply put, this is the premise that the store is responsible for the merchandising cycle or 4-step process to managing the items in each store. The order writer is the person closest to the customer and the sale of each item. By using the data collected, the order writer should make decisions on additions and deletions of products and how they are merchandised. Aggressive ordering, adjusting planograms and focus on top sellers and high potential new items, all relate to retailer initiative and owning the TK process, taking responsibility in heart, mind and soul.

Importantly, data collection started in our transformation to TK with manual handwritten order books. It was always the intent to mobilize electronic ordering and sales management that actually was not implemented until the mid to late 1990's. The logic was related to the monumental task of getting the entire North American leadership team and franchisees to understand and embrace TK fundamentals prior to the significant investment in electronic sales data collection and ordering. It was very important that we maintained "retailer initiative" in managing the business without allowing machines to make ordering decisions. It took several years to pass that test.

Also, with this, SEJ had significant success with fresh, daily delivered products leveraging partner suppliers in Japan. Over 60% of the SEJ products in the early 1990's were fresh, daily delivered items. This required an infrastructure with daily distribution partner companies that were interactive electronically with all store ordering. There was a big push on the part of SEJ to implement this massive business change in North America including fresh, daily delivered products. This strategic initiative was intended to help replace declining & lower margin cigarette, beer and bottle/can soft drinks that provide no competitive product differentiation.

Essentially, the fresh product initiative assured more sustainability in the highly competitive North American market.

Stepping back from what I know was a very difficult culture and business change nearly 30 years ago and witnessing the proven success of the TK business process– I feel fortunate and proud to have been part of it. I am grateful to the teams I worked with, the senior leaders and SEJ for the education I received. The best learning is practical learning and that the 7-Eleven experience was rich indeed. It has to go down as one of the most historic business turnarounds in North America.

Ultimately, the overriding strategy of TK is rooted in satisfying the customer. TK is a customer focused business process. Staying in stock of top selling items, introducing high potential new items and partnering with suppliers with an eye on differentiation enables high customer satisfaction. Again, the number one priority to a convenience customer is the ability to buy the item they want and need right now.

Taking Responsibility for Longevity Bolstered by *Tanpin Kanri*

Key Takeaways:
- ✓ *Strategy:* "Living in the Basics" and being in-stock on products customers want to buy through *Tanpin Kanri*.
- ✓ *Basic:* Retailer Initiative is closest to the customer and ordering is the #1 job of the store.
- ✓ *Execution:* Build a sustainable ordering process.
- ✓ *Execution:* Use the 4-step process that promotes constant improvement.
- ✓ *Execution:* Fresh, Daily Delivered Product implemented for incremental sales.

Repeatable Process

Tanpin Kanri (TK) places disciplined focus on the 4-step process to ensure 1) observation or current situational analysis; 2) hypothesis; 3) execution; and 4) review or data analysis with each item in the product mix. Attached to that is the "merchandising cycle" that differs by product category, supplier and even by item. For daily delivered items (fresh foods) the order window to delivery timeframe is under 24 hours. For other items (example: bottle & can beverages) the timeframe is one to two times per week delivery with a longer order to delivery window, sometimes over 24 hours, for the order writer to consider.

Item by item management, or TK, has a requirement to consider the order to delivery realities and to ensure order quantities are adequate for top sellers and high potential items and to avoid "missed opportunities." In the world of TK, proper execution of the 4-step process within the merchandising cycle should provide a high likelihood of success in maximizing sales of top sellers and high potential new items. The equivalent to this, using a baseball metaphor, is that the focus needs to be "base hits" not homeruns. TK is a strategy of incremental item sales growth.

Taking Responsibility for Repeatable Process

Key Takeaways:
- ✓ *Strategy:* Top Seller and High Potential Item focus promotes incremental sales growth.

✓ *Execution:* Implement the 4-step process and ensure that the Merchandising Cycle is managed effectively in the store(s).

Passion for Products that Matter Most

Fundamentally, in operating and leading a business successfully, prioritization and managing the vital money-making products is key. Using data to pinpoint trends clears the clutter and enables decision makers and order writers to spend 80% of their time on the top 20% of products that drive performance. This logic can be applied to the people management approach as well.

The TK process enables priority focus on products that customers want to buy. The "never, ever run out of top selling items" premise is job one for the 7-Eleven order writer. 7-Eleven deals in convenience and the ultimate convenience is having availability of products customers want or need to buy at all times. The reliability of this predicates the return visits that are necessary in the business concept and for success itself. Several examples of such items are 16-oz Lemon Lime Gatorade, Snickers single serve candy bars, 1-liter bottled water, 25-ounce Bud Light cans, Marlboro box cigarettes and Red Bull energy drink. Top sellers such as this list require abundant merchandising "facings" in the display placed in the most customer accessible part of the display or shelf.

Importantly, we aggressively deleted slow selling or dead items to free up space for top sellers and high potential new items. My good friend Joe Vonder Haar from Anheuser Busch worked closely with me to ensure items that were not producing at acceptable levels in the beer presentation were deleted. This partnership was great for both companies in using data to make product decisions. The top sellers and high potential items had the proper real estate in the presentation. Joe and I made numerous presentations together to our teams drilling down this data...very successfully!

Also, priority focus is placed on the high potential new items introduced in a weekly process managed at the headquarters level. The newest craft beer, nutritional bar, health-oriented beverage product or salty snack item, for example, are given the full support of the organization for merchandising in each store. Each store is asked to order such items and use the merchandising cycle and process to measure movement.

Essentially the growth opportunity leveraging a sustained process of measurement is foundational. Signage and merchandising that provides the customer visibility gives new, high potential products and categories a path to success. Significant partnering with suppliers and vendors gives 7-Eleven an edge in the competitive marketplace supported by TK and a unified 7-Eleven team.

Taking Responsibility for Passion for Products that Matter Most

Key Takeaways:
- ✓ *Strategy:* Priority focus on top selling items customers want to buy.
- ✓ *Execution:* Abundant merchandising of top sellers is implemented.
- ✓ *Execution:* New high potential items in-stock and fully implemented.
- ✓ *Execution:* Partnering with suppliers on new items for incremental sales and differentiation.

<u>Four P's: Product, Placement, Presentation and Promotion</u>

Classic Marketing 101 emphasizes the "4 P's" of retail selling at the store level for products offered. Sales plans using TK, and the 4 P's, help empower the store manager and store team to take charge of sales and grow the business. Throughout my retail management career, most specifically at 7-Eleven, I used check-points as a cue in my head to ensure the "memorable" 4 P's had effective plans and actions with each. This gave us the best chance of maximizing sales of top selling and high potential items. The following are considerations when executing the 4 P's:

- ✓ **Product** – right item in size, color, trend that can be fully available from suppliers and to the customer.

- ✓ **Placement** – high traffic location, strong visibility at eye level with easy access for the customer on the selling floor or in the display.
- ✓ **Presentation** – abundant with product and attractive with well-organized, clean displays and clear information on the offer to engage the customer.
- ✓ **Promotion** – Compelling, clear and prominent signage that conveys price and offer that informs customer of value.

Maniacal use of Data and Facts

Retailers, food and beverage managers, and perhaps most operators in business are predisposed to action. Analysis of data and using the left side of the brain is not the first inclination. At 7-Eleven, the habit to make decisions using data on product was developed over a long period of time. We spent years, and for many of us whole careers, using intuitive abilities to make decisions on product assortment and promotions to propel the business. Pen and paper analysis were mainly "rear view mirror" of what happened instead of using data to help plan for what could be. When the backward focus or results regurgitation failed in the late 1980's, the organization required the strong use of data and facts to prepare hypothesis and models of planning for success going forward.

Decision making in any business or organization should have a strong reliance on facts and objective data to ensure it succeeds. This notion applies to any key decision-making process – not just marketing. Too often, laziness and charismatic impulses lead to poor decisions that put the very survival of companies and the jobs of people at risk. 7-Eleven is the best example of this in my career, but each company I was part of had these challenges. Leaders should demand rigorous data and analysis in every key decision.

Taking Responsibility for Maniacal use of Data and Facts

Key Takeaways:
- ✓ *Strategy:* Reinforce a culture that relies on facts and data.
- ✓ *Basic:* A rigorous analysis of data is the responsibility of top leaders.
- ✓ *Execution:* 30% backward analysis and 70% forward looking is the ordering thought process.

Constantly Adjust and Modify

The disciplined use of facts and data to make product decisions leads to a collection of information that is organized daily, weekly and monthly. At 7-Eleven, we started collecting data in manual order books laid out by order cycle. Over time this manual process led to the eventual development of an electronic sales management hardware and process that captured individual item sales real-time at the store and headquarters. It was state of the art and trailblazing for a chain the size of 7-Eleven. Importantly, however, the data collection enabled human decision making on product ordering, which was not relegated to auto replenishment.

Adjusting and modifying orders of top sellers and high potential items empowers the store order writer to take action and drive sales based on sound judgment using facts. Many retailing organizations have systemized ordering with auto-replenishment, which relies on the machine. There are many pitfalls of auto-replenishment resulting from inaccurate data, errors, product theft and other conditions in retail. Human order writers making judgments on order quantity demonstrated great success over long periods at 7-Eleven.

TK is about "Retailer Initiative," which is fundamentally taking responsibility for your business. For your customers, the mission is to have the right products in the "right place at the right time." 7-Eleven transformed a failing business model into a winning business strategy that has now succeeded for nearly 3 decades. Constantly adjusting and modifying the ordering focus to stay in stock on top sellers, eliminating slow sellers and introducing high potential new items saved 7-Eleven. It is roll up your sleeves hard work that pays off.

Taking Responsibility to Constantly Adjust and Modify

Key Takeaways:

✓ *Strategy:* Human decision making on ordering is fundamental to the sales growth model.
✓ *Basic:* Data and facts support sound ordering decisions.
✓ *Basic:* Auto replenishment has many pitfalls (not strategic priority at 7-Eleven for good reason).
✓ *Execution:* Fully train and monitor the performance of order-writers and management by store.

Chapter Four

Culture of Responsibility (Heart & Mind)

Taking Responsibility for the business or organization is more than just the work of the leader. It requires a common purpose or "culture" that has every stakeholder mobilized with the same spirit and goals. The stakeholders include every manager and employee, suppliers and vendors, financial investors and supporters and the customers (yes, the customers). When the stakeholders in a company have passion for the product, mission statement and guiding principles, the customers notice and take their experience and product personally.

The culture of 7-Eleven and Starbucks could not be more different from a mission statement point of view. The two companies operated completely differently, though successfully. Each of these companies, both of which I know very well, stand for the needs of their customers and the entire organization is clear on what "right" looks like.

At 7-Eleven, the ultimate customer service is ensuring the products the customer wants to buy are available, reasonably priced and transacted quickly and easily. The store environment should be clean, safe and the store clerk should be courteous. If this happens, most of the time, with 800-1000 transactions per day, 7-

Eleven is working as a culture. The track record indicates sustainable results since the business transformation in the 1980's.

At Starbucks, the customer service expectation is high touch to create a feeling of "my store, my drink" and as often as possible, "legendary experiences" for customers. Training time and focus is on interactions between baristas and customers with a "say yes" approach to service with the premium priced beverages being prepared. The store is a gathering place to inspire togetherness and community– the company culture is strongly influenced to that end and Starbucks has been extremely successful in achieving these objectives over decades.

The common link between 7-Eleven and Starbucks is that both companies have a longstanding culture that mobilized stakeholders to succeed by working together. To me, the learning is profound. I learned that understanding product strategy at 7-Eleven and witnessing thousands of people executing that strategy with passion and purpose drove incredible volume and success. The key: a sound product strategy executed well can be overwhelmingly successful.

At Starbucks, I learned that a world-class people strategy as the primary focus of a passionate leadership team is life-changing. The business concept of coffee shops on the corner was not new. But great, internationally sourced and well-roasted coffee with the artistic flair in preparation that inspired conversation, led to a new differentiation. The marketplace has been permanently changed by Starbucks. This chapter is devoted to understanding the great impact of company culture and adjacently how that culture influences responsibility for process and results.

Ownership by Every Team Member

Great companies and organizations have everybody on the team treating the business as if they own it with a personal vested interest, taking responsibility- heart, mind and soul. They hire the right people with character, along with, ample talents. They message frequently what they stand for and what "right" looks like. They have a passion for the customer and an ability to see the service they provide from a customer's point of view. With all of this, the sense of responsibility to meet or exceed the customer promise and/or expectations is uncompromising. There is an emotional connection between each team member and the company that translates to high standards of execution.

Attention to the details of the business translates to constantly improving process and the ability to achieve high customer satisfaction and efficiencies to manage costs effectively. No company or organization can balance that act well to be successful without a great sense of personal responsibility from each team member.

Most companies have many moving parts and in order to ensure that customers receive the product or service at or above expectation, there must be effective communication. Great repeatable process, with engaged and motivated people, influences effective communication.

The best examples in the fast food arena today are Chick Fil A and In N Out Burger. Rarely, if ever, do customers encounter a poor experience. Both of these chains deliver on the promise and you can feel the hustle and drive of every smiling team member in every routine visit. Compare these chains to McDonald's and KFC and you will see the difference in "ownership." No longer are the traditional businesses that were considered stalwart purveyors coming close to the standard of excellence displayed by Chick Fil A and In N Out Burger. Customers feel the ownership of these businesses. Interestingly, Chick Fil A delivers with a well-run franchise model that is connected robustly with the company mission. In N Out is a well-run 100% corporate run operation. Different models with very satisfied regular customers. Great, passionate leadership and team members with delighted customers are the cornerstone elements.

Taking Responsibility for Ownership by Every Team Member

Key Takeaways:
- ✓ *Strategy:* Store operators act as owners with associated empowerment and compensation plans.
- ✓ *Basic:* Great teams have people that show a personal vested interest.
- ✓ *Execution:* Train and develop store managers to lead and manage details of store operation to the expectation of uncompromising standards.
- ✓ *Execution:* Implement highly competitive compensation plans that reward high performance.
- ✓ *Execution:* Weekly, monthly communication that highlights successful and below par performance to share learning and drive results.

Sniffing out Excuses Coaching in the Moment

Taking responsibility requires good listening skills and *really* hearing what members of the team are saying. A former boss of mine once told me the most important part of effective semantics is listening. This is a very insightful. Striving to listen in conversations at least 70% of the time is a sound a rule of thumb. The key to this rule means asking questions and patiently listening before responding. In order to coach and help solve problems, it is key to fully understand the facts in each interaction.

In order to create, nurture and facilitate a culture of responsibility, "sniffing out excuses" with individuals on the team is imperative. Questionable decision-making, ineffective programs and sub-par performance of team members will create easy excuses and blame for poor results. To hold high standards of success in that culture of responsibility, the leader must make every effort to drive out excuses. Blame-fixing and excuse-making will destroy team spirit and ultimately the success of the team and organization.

When a leader hears an individual on the team deflect or rationalize poor performance, it requires some probing to bring out the underlying reasons for the lack of responsibility being projected. There is not a good reason to "dance around" what is being excused and dismissed. This is something that needs to be addressed quickly to firmly resolve who is responsible for the work, results and outcome. It should end with agreement on clear responsibility for the work and commitments to improve and take the performance to acceptable levels.

Signals sent very clearly from the leader on the expectations and standards for the business or organization, in real time, reinforce the mission of the team. This must be continuous and passionate to lead high performing teams. It is not personal and is always in the best interest of being the very best team it can be.

Taking Responsibility for Sniffing out Excuses
Coaching in the Moment

Key Takeaways:
- ✓ *Strategy:* Ensure effective communication to overcome obstacles.
- ✓ *Basic:* Reinforce strong listening skills at all levels as a culture.
- ✓ *Execution:* Address excuse-making directly and quickly by probing questions.
- ✓ *Execution:* Agree on accountability for the work.
- ✓ *Execution:* Ensure commitments are made to resolve sub-par performance.

Proactively Helping Others

A culture of responsibility is fostered and strengthened by helping others on the team during difficult periods. Smooth sailing in business is fleeting. Anybody that doesn't face adversity is either kidding themselves or headed for an unpleasant surprise. The best teammates are the ones that recognize and offer assistance generously before they are asked, or before a crisis arises. The best teams have several of those individuals. I have been fortunate to be part of those type of teams most of my career.

My brother Bill is 16 months younger than I am. Bill and I grew up alongside each other and he always had my back and I always had his. We took responsibility for each other. We "proactively helped" one another.

Bill is the perfect complement to me in personality because he seems to have strengths in all the areas where I have weaknesses. Throughout our lives we have leveraged this quite often to draw strength and wisdom and make our sum total better.

Bill has carried the mission of "proactively helping others" with significant personal commitment to aiding the terminally ill. He has routinely provided comfort, conversation and prayer with those suffering at a hospital near his home. These suffering people have drawn strength from Bill's acts of kindness.

Bill lost his wife Katie to brain cancer at age 47 in 2006. He and his two young daughters experienced an unimaginable time most of us would not fully comprehend. The work he has been doing with the afflicted at the hospital is the embodiment of "proactively helping others." This is an extraordinary example of taking personal experience and giving back to others, taking responsibility in heart, mind and soul.

Very early on at 7-Eleven, I learned that helping others meant the difference between success and failure of the team. We operated in a franchise area that was not tailored staff-wise, to run corporate stores while attending to the responsibilities we had with our franchisees. However, there were frequent periods where 4, 5 or 6 corporate stores cropped up due to unsuccessful franchising efforts. In an average district that meant each of us had at least 1 corporate store or more.

Operating a 24-hour store – hiring, controlling losses and shrinkage, merchandising and all other aspects of that store, along with additional franchise operations, made the workload overwhelming. This usually called for a 6-7 day per week schedule without much free time. I never knew how much I could appreciate the colleague next to me until I faced these challenges. I also became very aware of the importance of helping when I saw others in the same position.

Whether it was staff shortages requiring hiring efforts with interviewing, training and coaching, or dealing with negative audit results from employee theft, there were challenges that could severely impair the financial results of corporate run stores. These are losses that meant the difference between making goal, receiving a bonus or even keeping your job. It was a world of high stress, very hard work and a long list of priorities. We needed each other to prioritize the priorities.

7-Eleven had, in general, a great group of leaders that influenced the spirit of teamwork. Rarely were there folks that didn't carry the spirit of team and were absent in the times of challenges. Culturally, it was not accepted and usually those individuals did not last long. Helping others was fundamentally the social norm in the operation of the business. This mindset and approach were embedded in every role I had as a colleague and leader throughout my career.

Taking Responsibility for Proactively Helping Others

Key Takeaways:
- ✓ *Strategy:* A culture of responsibility that promotes helping colleagues proactively.
- ✓ *Basic:* Periods of adversity are unavoidable.
- ✓ *Execution:* Prioritizing the priorities is needed in times of challenge.

Situational Leadership

In 2003 – 2004, Starbucks introduced *Situational Leadership* workshops for store managers and the leadership teams across North America in the roughly 12,000 stores at the time. My region was one of 13 where this "language" or process was implemented. Dr. Paul Hersey developed the *Situational Leadership* Model in the 1960's, which he called "organized common sense." The Model has endured over 50 years and the *Center for Leadership Studies* in Southern California is an institution with an outstanding reputation.

Situational Leadership is facilitated by corporate leaders, trainers and facilitators that travel to the *Center for Leadership Studies* near San Diego for certification to take back to their organizations, which in our case was Starbucks. So, we had in house Starbucks facilitators that led 2-3-day workshops for store managers, field leaders and other staff support leaders.

The *Situational Leadership* Model was invaluable to me as a senior leader to help get over 500 stores and district managers to consciously and effectively lead and manage people. Use of tried and true techniques that have been proven over time empowers leaders to develop their skills with a trusted roadmap. These are basic skills that have consistent terms and techniques, which are very meaningful in operating chain stores or multi-unit locations.

The premise of *Situational Leadership* is considering the willingness, ability and skills of the employee in getting the tasks accomplished effectively in daily work. There are 4 Leadership Styles of the boss relating to 4 Performance Readiness levels of the employee. Simply, for the boss, you learn what level of readiness for performance exists for employees being managed. The 4 ranges of Readiness require the boss to flex. The model helps analyze the proper approach from hands on to hands off in addressing employee need for direction.

In 2003–2004, I had over 25 years of experience in leading medium sized to very large organizations. The *Situational Leadership* Model took me personally to the next level of understanding how to connect the dots with my teams. Just the terminology alone, of which I saw consistent use at Starbucks, enabled the organization to more efficiently and effectively lead. I found it to be a game changer during a time when we were building stores, hiring aggressively and seeing double-digit growth in existing business. We greatly needed this to be thoughtful in our leadership practices.

I am such an advocate of the *Situational Leadership* Model that I introduced it to my 100 dental offices and field teams in 2011 at Smile Brands. Again, we were building new offices and growing the practices in revenue at nearly double-digit clips at that time. Situational Leadership helped standardize our approach and led to a better functioning team.

Taking Responsibility to implement Situational Leadership

Key Takeaways:
- ✓ *Strategy: Situational Leadership* model to develop skills of all leaders and standardize process of development with common language.
- ✓ *Execution:* 2-3 Day Workshops led by "certified" in-house Leaders.
- ✓ *Execution:* Leadership skill development implemented in work environment post-workshop.
- ✓ *Execution:* Leader or boss flexes to needs of direction (readiness) of employees.

A Learning Organization

Moving from a retail/food & beverage leadership career after over 30 years to a healthcare/dental services company was very rich and rewarding, but it was also an extremely challenging pursuit. This decision was primarily grounded in the desire to stretch my leadership abilities and contribute to a growth-oriented model in a completely different sector. The primary motivator to make the change was my strong impression that Smile Brands was a learning organization.

In very short order, it became clear to me that my region team, mainly homegrown dental operational managers, were limited in their exposure to leadership. The company and dental sector had a task driven culture that I found hard-edged. The team as a group had excellent technical abilities related to dentistry, quality assurance and ensuring patient care was safe and solid. However, interpersonal skills and treating each other respectfully was lacking. In the first year or two, my mission as a leader was to identify leaders on my team with the style to help me soften the hard edge and create a new culture of respect.

It was important to help coach and develop a few senior leaders on my team that had all the "heart" to be examples and advocates for servant leadership. At the same time, there were others on my team that lacked the willingness or ability to change. Unfortunately, though the majority possessed great dental acumen, changes were necessary to elevate the culture of respect and spirit of leadership development. Changes in the make-up of the team would be required.

It was a difficult period, but we were creating a learning organization that showed a quantum leap in the first two years. The team consistently improved in the subsequent 5 years of the time at Smile Brands. This experience, which frankly many times made me feel like a "fish out of water," brought the rewards of seeing people grow exponentially. At the same time, I experienced and faced being uncomfortable as a leader throughout the process. Having said that, it was a chance of a lifetime and privilege to work with an excellent group of people.

Taking Responsibility for A Learning Organization

Key Takeaways:
- ✓ *Strategy:* Developing leaders enriches a Learning Organization.
- ✓ *Basic:* Welcome being uncomfortable in leading culture change.
- ✓ *Execution:* Embrace change from Retail/Food & Beverage to Healthcare services by actively embracing need for new sector education.
- ✓ *Execution:* Softening hard-edge culture by creating significant change in communication.

Accountability for Results

Being responsible as a leader in business or any organization is predicated on fully owning the results produced, or not produced, by the team. By results, I am referring to hitting numerical or budget goals and consistently showing improvement in the quantifiable or measurable work managed by the team. Successful leaders and teams deliver results that are compared to budgets, previous year or quarter and other regions or markets.

Much of what has been discussed thus far in the book is an overview of process to develop the best people, teams, systems and repeatable routines. In my view, all of those elements, executed well, give the best possible chance of success in leading a multi-location business. At the same time, the "bottom-line is the bottom-line" and the leader cannot lose sight of that reality. Tolerating poor results is not the behavior of financial investors, CEO's or other senior leaders or boards guiding companies and organizations. That is rightfully how it works in the real world.

Poor performance in measurable results, should never be rationalized or excused away by responsible leaders or teams. There should be no excuses, ever. Taking Responsibility in heart, mind and soul for below par results and having a genuine sense of urgency to modify direction and mobilize the team to act is the hallmark of a good leader. Below par results are inevitable with every leader's work and it *will* happen. But, with this, the response to turn the situation around with an urgent, detailed action plan, without being prompted by the boss, is healthy leadership. Being proactive rather than reactive to drive results, most ensures positive, expedient outcomes.

Senior Leaders, CEO's, Boards and Executive Committees relish supporting proactive leaders. "Managing up" is also good functional leadership. Constructing action plans and mobilizing the team to execute, without being prompted, demonstrates that the people responsible are in command. The Leader should absolutely loop in the senior leaders and welcome feedback and advice on the steps/actions being taken to address results. By communicating effectively, the leader is giving firm signals that the sub-par results are being addressed. This elevates confidence and opportunity to make the actions even more effective through good communication and fact-based dialogue. This is functional problem-solving.

Subscribing to the "all hands-on-deck" mindset to nail expected results, all of the time, gives the leader a robust and "get it done" culture. Leading people to confidently be the best in measurable results, engenders the best of team spirit and loyalty. To me this is what sense of urgency means as a key part of taking responsibility in heart, mind and soul.

Taking Responsibility for Accountability for Results

Key Takeaways:
- ✓ *Strategy:* 'Hitting the Numbers' and owning the responsibility for results.
- ✓ *Basic:* No excuse for missing measurable result targets.
- ✓ *Execution:* Sense of urgency to address missing targets.
- ✓ *Execution:* Communicate proactively with the senior team.

<u>Getting Things Done</u>

Successful people learn, adjust and constantly strive to improve to be the best they can be in their work and in life. I do not equate the term "strive" to the term "try." I see the word strive as a determined focus that has a successful outcome expected. "Try" is word that has evolved into the notion that it will be acceptable and tolerable to miss the objective. Words matter in leading teams and the clarity with regard to my point here is important in taking responsibility.

My brother Jim is eight years older than me. He is the most organized, disciplined and hardworking individual I have ever known. Jim, an Eagle Scout, took responsibility as the father figure to Bill and me almost immediately after my dad left our family when I was 8 and Bill was 7 years old. He became the major support to my mom and shouldered transportation duties, school event support, little league, along with all the other mentoring needed to help second and third grade kids keep it together. Jim was living in our house, going to school and working the whole time until he graduated college and was drafted into the National Guard at age 22. Jim lives "getting things done."

After several years of working with a large multi-national accounting firm Jim and his wife established what is now a highly successful 35-year accounting practice, and they did this while raising 2 successful men together.

My younger brother Bill and I benefited greatly from Jim's leadership and sense of responsibility rooted in a very caring but tough love. He taught us important lessons in "getting things done" that each of us have drawn on to nail important accomplishments in work and life. Jim is an extraordinary example of taking responsibility in everything he does.

Early on in my career at 7-Eleven, a favorite leader of mine often asked the team for a "relentless and determined" approach to getting things done. That phrase is etched in my mind in everything I do that is a priority and embodies a mindset of constant improvement. This defines the passion that successful people take to their work in leading teams. Take on important matters with an "all-in" mentality and start every initiative with the end in mind. This leads to the pay-off of getting better every day in sustained success and the rewards, and that benefits all involved.

Think about exceptional people you know that are successful in their lives. The passion for getting better every day will be a characteristic they share. These people look at adversity as a challenge, they communicate in a specific and clear way, they are objective and self-critical, and their spirit is never broken. It all ties back to taking responsibility in heart, mind and soul.

Taking Responsibility for Getting Things Done

Key Takeaways:
- ✓ *Strategy:* Mobilize exceptional people that "get things done."
- ✓ *Basic:* "Striving" and "Trying" have different meanings.
- ✓ *Execution:* Relentless and determined approach to dig into details, set goals and monitor results frequently.

Chapter Five

<u>Serving Your People (Soul)</u>

Having values that are centered around people on the team and serving them enthusiastically is the "soul" of the business or organization. Many describe this mindset or "way of being" as an upside-down pyramid or hierarchy. Instead of the leader or boss directing, instructing or dictating orders from the top to get the job done, they create an environment of openness and deference to the team and customer in facilitating effective work. In many ways, it is a sense or inclination, to help others succeed. The best leader as a servant will humbly take responsibility for their team of people as the highest priority. Effectiveness in the work and results coming from the work will emanate from the virtue of this service to others.

This approach to leadership is no longer unconventional. However, there are many that profess servant leadership as a mantra but simply fail in executing or truly embracing it as a way of being. The "go to" approach of giving direction and using positional authority to complete tasks is often the reality for organizations with big titles, big offices and where the fountain of knowledge is anywhere but close to the customer. This may sound cynical but the need to depend on power and resources from investors, and other key financial stakeholders, may doom servant leadership. A servant leader plays the long game with belief in the principle of serving the team. External forces, like investors, that should also benefit from the tenets of servant leadership, must be stewarded with proper leadership and communication of company leaders. This takes courage and commitment.

I learned servant leadership as I was growing up before anybody wrote about it. It was unofficial. I learned it from my brother Steve.

Steve is 5 years older than I am. He is the most compassionate, caring, generous, and resourceful person I have ever known. Steve fought for and protected the family, especially his younger brothers, all along the way during some extremely tumultuous times.

Throughout his life, Steve is the guy that considers others first and fights for the underdog or underprivileged. Steve has been a Trustee and Board Member at the University of San Francisco the past 10 years in helping the university educate young people. USF is where he received his law degree and he is generously giving back.

Steve had a huge influence on me in my college days where I struggled. He coached me to enroll in College of the Canyons in Valencia, California when I missed the mark on a 4-year option based on my sub-par high school academics. He knew I was tortured over my missteps and immaturity in high school. I later attended and graduated from St. Mary's College with a degree. He has had his hand in several career decisions I have made, and his guidance is extremely valuable as he pushed me to be uncomfortable and realize my full potential. He has a servant's heart.

When I received a cancer diagnosis while working for Starbucks in China in 2007, it was Steve I called to help me get it together emotionally and otherwise. When I woke up at City of Hope in Duarte, California, after having treatment and surgery, Steve was the first person I saw seated near my wife Kathy. Every family member in crisis seems to turn to Steve and he is always there. Steve is an exceptional human being that model's servant leadership in taking responsibility with heart, mind and soul.

Servant Leadership as a Basic

The *Servant Leader*, a book by James A. Autry, has been used by a great number of companies and organizations over the past 20 years to help create a functional culture. At Starbucks, we used this book in workshops, trainings and as a daily reference to help drill the mission and guiding principles that mirrored the premise of the servant leader. Starbucks decidedly embraced "serving each other" before I joined the company in 2002, and it was alive throughout my 6 plus years. It was a remarkable period in my career because of the genuine commitment to the spirit of the servant leader throughout the organization.

Every leader or aspiring leader should read the *Servant Leader*. It is an easy read that highlights and drills the "Five Ways of Being" as fundamental to effective and functional leadership. The book gives helpful structure on "how to build a creative team, develop great morale, and improve bottom-line performance."

The 5 Ways of Being Pathway

The *Servant Leader* is grounded in the Five Ways of Being that embody characteristics of the leader as a servant. Importantly, these are foundational behaviors that provide the leader with recognizable and coachable elements that impact the entire organization.

The following is a recap of the Five Ways of Being:
- *Be Authentic*
  Be who you are.
- *Be Vulnerable*
  Be empathetic, humble and honest with feelings.
- *Be Accepting*
  Be open & respectful to others' points of view and resist picking winners and losers.
- *Be Present*
  Be part of the process and actively engage without distraction.

- *Be Useful*
    Be a helpful resource to others.

Some folks resist the notion of "being soft," or consider the servant leader basics as "psychobabble." I believe the opposite. To live the Five Ways of Being as a leader or just in daily life is a process of courage. These are practical principles that influence productive and positive decisions and outcomes. These principles are easily stated and understood but very difficult to live as values. Again, this takes courage and conviction and it changes lives.

Taking Responsibility to implement Servant Leadership as a Basic

Key Takeaways:
- ✓ *Strategy: The Servant Leader* by James A. Autry
- ✓ *Basic:* Foundational Process of Leadership
- ✓ *Execution:* Five Ways of Being characteristics

Starbucks Guiding Principles

Starbucks constantly reinforces the guiding principles of the company mission statement with every employee or "Partner" in all forums. The resources and training materials are routinely connected to those guiding principles to live the values of the company, whether as a part time barista in a store, or as a senior vice president in the headquarters ("support center") office. There has never been any experience, with any of the companies I have worked for or with that had such a genuinely connected message related to what the organization stands for.

Starbucks' mission and guiding principles, in many aspects put into action the "ways of being" as highlighted in the previous section for *The Servant Leader*.

The Mission and Guiding Principles of Starbucks Coffee Company are as follows (minor changes since my time at Starbucks, but Mission has not changed):

Mission – *To Inspire and Nurture the Human Spirit*

Guiding Principles or *Values*

- *Creating a culture of warmth and belonging where everyone is welcome.*
- *Acting with courage, challenging the status quo and finding new ways to grow our company and each other.*
- *Being Present, connecting with transparency.*
- *Delivering our best in all we do, holding ourselves accountable for results.*
- *We are performance driven, through the lens of humanity.*

It is a general practice for most companies to create mission statement documents that provide noble and even heartfelt guidelines to define its purpose. Unfortunately, in most cases, the majority of the company's employees, stakeholders and even senior management, are unable to recite part or all of the mission. The result of this is a very broad array of important companies that lack a soul that connects all of its stakeholders, including customers. This is a limitless opportunity for leaders in every company to be part of the best growth engine I was fortunate enough to be part of at Starbucks.

Taking Responsibility to reinforce Mission and Guiding Principles

Key Takeaways:
- ✓ *Strategy:* Mission Statements and Guiding Principles fully communicated, understood and embraced as "why we are here."
- ✓ *Execution:* Every company meeting should start with review of Mission Statement and Guiding Principles.
- ✓ *Execution:* Review performance on all key imperatives matched against the Mission Statement.

Attitude is a Choice

I will never forget the sign on the office credenza of my boss at Starbucks that read simply "Choose Your Attitude." I think this straightforward phrase embodies what taking responsibility means. The first accountability a person has is to themselves. In order to serve others effectively requires the genuine willingness to influence, lead by example and ultimately motivate others with a "can do" spirit that reflects in attitude.

Everyone has been around people that can change the tone of a meeting, project, work atmosphere or even a simple interaction by their demeanor and approach. This can be done in 3 distinctly different ways:

- **Positive and constructive** – open, welcoming and inclusive in dialogue that builds relationships and helps solves problems. This is the "glass half full" attitude and usually gets stuff done.
- **Skeptical and cynical** – sees the problems first, leans toward doubt in dialogue, is likely moody and blames others when things don't go as planned. This is the "glass half empty" attitude and can help keep things real to refine a work product.
- **Indifferent** – goes with the flow and let's others take the lead. Doesn't commit to anything unless pushed. This is a "wishy washy" attitude that must be managed by others to ensure the job gets done.

Teams normally have a mix of personalities and attitudes. Leaders have the responsibility to spot the three types I have identified and properly leverage or manage people effectively to get the job done. Look for the "positive and constructive" attitudes to take charge of priorities and help teams and projects ascend through their guidance and leadership.

At 7-Eleven we would convene monthly Market

Manager meetings to plan the execution of company and local initiatives for Division. This meeting also included store staff support leaders from merchandising, human resources, training, security, service maintenance and a few others. As the Division leader, I chaired the meetings. The work expected to serve the stores and the Field Leaders, was to produce a specific plan of communication and execution for new products and promotions for upcoming periods.

With 12 Market Managers there was a mix of positive, cynical and indifferent attitudes. Given this, I developed 3 breakout groups led by my strongest, largely positive attitude managers who I had assigned. Each group would be charged with developing execution plans to present to the larger group for discussion, consensus and confirmation. When we left the meeting and had all opinions vetted, we would communicate this to the field team and stores for execution as the complete plan.

The most important work was to ensure that the breakout teams were well-designed for active participation and a mix of experience and attitude. The accountability for the plan relied on the breakout group working together on a work product that passed the test of the whole group. This also enabled me to monthly assess the development of individuals on my team and quality of peer leadership. This aspect is a great measure of how the individual is "choosing their attitude." It was the most fundamentally important day of working together each month to serve our teams and each other. This is taking responsibility in heart, mind and soul.

Taking Responsibility to reinforce Attitude is a Choice

Key Takeaways:
- ✓ *Strategy:* Lead the team to productivity serving each other and the larger group.
- ✓ *Execution:* "Choose your Attitude" communicated as the premise for productive dialogue and reinforced.
- ✓ *Execution:* Spot 3 different attitudes of team members.

Never "Walk By" Sub-standard Customer Imperatives

At Starbucks I learned a key way to influence and lead people to execute "uncompromising" standards of serving customers. With this, I heard our CEO discuss the notion of ignoring unacceptable behaviors and poor execution of Starbucks policies and programs in stores. Simply by ignoring such behaviors and execution in store visits or "walking by" below standard examples, a leader has given tacit approval to it. This really resonated with me. It was a call to action to be a standard bearer of uncompromising Starbucks standards. I built it into my mindset and routine for critically observing and acting on this message.

Starbucks has a wide range of significant customer focused execution priorities. Of course, cleanliness standards throughout the store have a long list of expectations that are consistent in most food and beverage purveyors. But, to me that is the easy stuff, as most of those issues are clear and can be easily ticked off and addressed quickly. Restrooms or floors, tables, chairs and counters are either clean or not. Working with a store team to make these responsibilities routine is straightforward.

The more pressing piece requiring strong observation, are the behaviors related to customer interaction and beverage quality. Starbucks provides a premium product at a premium price. The customer expectation is a product delivered to their customized liking and satisfaction in a friendly and engaging manner. If this does not happen or becomes "transactional" the uncompromising standard is not met. Taking responsibility for the behavior of the barista at the counter is key to any Starbucks leader.

In my store visits, I would find ways to observe the "moment of truth" related to the customer interaction and the preparation of beverages. With customer service, just sitting in the lobby and watching several customer transactions gave me points of feedback for the Store Manager. The specific examples drawn from these observations helped a healthy dialogue on how we are doing in engaging with our customers. We all knew the standards, and this helped model and reinforce meeting or exceeding the high bar.

With beverage standards, I would order a drink and taste and see that it was made to standard. I liked ordering a cappuccino as it requires "tight" foam, without visible bubbles, to present the best of what Starbucks does. If the foam was right, I knew the barista was trained well and executing effectively. It gave me a great chance to serve by complementing them and reinforcing the standard. If coaching was needed, I did so as a teacher in a helpful way, also a reinforcing leadership technique.

Not "walking by" substandard execution and behaviors is critical to be a strong standard bearer as a servant leader. Taking responsibility in heart, mind and soul is served greatly by this mindset.

Taking Responsibility to Never "Walk By" Sub-standard Customer Imperatives

Key Takeaways:
- ✓ *Strategy:* Leader is the standard bearer and teacher.
- ✓ *Execution:* Never "walk by" and give tacit approval to sub-standard execution.
- ✓ *Execution:* Closely observe examples of execution and behavior and give immediate feedback.

An Effective Coaching Conversation

Taking responsibility and being present and useful by serving the team requires effective and active coaching. Being present means noticing the good and the bad with regard to the work of the team. Being useful requires a communication that helps the individual and the team improve. To serve effectively, as long as the coaching is not about an urgent problem, it is always helpful to compliment an individual on the work they are doing, and any special behaviors being observed. From there, "asking why" related to specific observations will help the coach discover the reason the individual is not performing a task or customer interaction to standard. The learning may help coach others in the same situation.

Making a coaching conversation into a discussion of understanding, rather than criticism, prevents the natural defensiveness or sensitivity to feedback. To serve effectively, good listening is absolutely required in coaching an individual and a team in general. This requires patience and humility. Stylistically, many leaders will struggle with this.

With more urgent problems that are grossly sub-standard, there is not time to have a coaching conversation. It is absurd to pretend a good coaching conversation would be the proper approach while

"Rome is burning." The leader approach in that case requires action to immediately fix the sub-standard condition and discover the causes at a later time- with good listening and problem solving to serve the team well.

Taking Responsibility for An Effective Coaching Conversation

Key Takeaways:
- ✓ *Strategy:* Encourage rich coaching that is leader-led to lift up team.
- ✓ *Execution:* Be present and useful in coaching individuals and the team.
- ✓ *Execution:* "Ask why" to discover reasons and solutions.
- ✓ *Execution:* Make coaching a discussion.
- ✓ *Execution:* Grossly sub-standard situations require urgent action and *then* coaching.

Sometimes Parting Ways is Serving

Taking responsibility requires the leader to serve others, including those on the team that lack the willingness or the skill to elevate the work of the team. Responsible leaders should be loyal to each individual team member they are serving. However, it is not serving the team when *blind* loyalty creeps in and the customer and work product are allowed to erode due to the sub-standard work of an individual.

Teams elevate and business circumstances evolve. At

times, individual team members that were high performing in the past, decline in performance and productivity when measured against peers. What once was in the best interest of the team, becomes a problem that must be addressed. Fairness and effective coaching conversations should be exhaustive to improve and elevate performance to acceptable levels for such individuals. Objective and measurable goals should be set and achieved.

When, in some cases, reasonable expectations and timeframes are not met by individuals, the leader must take responsibility to serve the team and individual. The leader must communicate that the performance plan is not achieving the goals and action must be taken to separate the individual from the company or organization. This difficult process is necessary in every organization and is inevitable for any responsible servant leader.

The outcome of this action will serve the team by giving other individuals the opportunity to elevate the experience of the customer and performance of the team. At the same time, the individual is freed of a difficult situation to pursue changes, that in many cases elevates their future. This is one of the most difficult realities of taking responsibility in heart, mind and soul with regard to servant leadership.

A Servant's Heart...A Serving Culture

Taking responsibility effectively and with purpose requires the heart of a servant. With this, in my experience, it also requires the mind of a servant. The combination of serving with heart and mind in taking responsibility as a leader will construct the *soul* of the team. Helping others, putting the team first, high ethics, humility, hard work and high performance are all consistent virtues related to the soul of such a team. This becomes a way of life and sensibility as the team works together for a while and emanates from the leader imperatives.

A servant's heart is grounded in love for the individuals and the team, much like a family. Anything good that comes from the work of the team, starts with the emotional side and that is heart. If we were machines, this would not matter. But thankfully we are not machines, and the recognition of taking responsibility in heart, mind and soul requires a serving culture. To believe and lead in this mindset, love of the individual and the team is cornerstone.

Taking Responsibility for A Servant's Heart...A Serving Culture

Key Takeaways:
- ✓ *Strategy:* Heart, mind and soul is about love of the individual and the team.

- ✓ *Basic:* Leading with purpose requires the heart of a servant.
- ✓ *Execution:* Leader constantly reinforces servant leadership as a way of being.

Chapter Six

Putting it all Together
(Heart, Mind and Soul)

The 2001 Book *Good to Great* by Jim Collins is a study of successful companies and the leadership benchmarks and people that got them there. Essentially, there are 5 levels of leadership described in the book with *Level 5* as Executive. Collins describes the *Level 5 Leader* as someone who "builds enduring greatness through a paradoxical blend of personal humility and professional will."

The *Level 5* leader described in *Good to Great* takes responsibility with heart, mind and soul. Collins emphasizes an important aspect that clearly matters in a big way- *discipline. Disciplined People, Disciplined Thought*, and *Disciplined Action* of these *Level 5* Leaders produce a "Flywheel" effect that creates "Breakthrough" performance. Having read and subscribed to the well-documented success stories in Jim Collins book eighteen years ago, I have seen further evidence in the teams with whom I've been fortunate to have been a part.

Taking responsibility in heart, mind and soul requires belief in the discipline of repeatable routine and striving to do things as a team the right way. To use a baseball analogy, this is about base hits not homeruns and relies on the team not one or two top players. In a sense it is playing the odds that a group of well-trained and developed good performers will succeed more consistently than a group of average people with one or two high performers.

Importantly, being relentless and determined to stay on plan and build momentum on the *fly wheel* leads to sustained success. The key message Jim Collins imparts is the notion of belief in the plan and disciplined execution of the plan. The proven examples of successfully run companies substantiates *"Good to Great"* with facts.

This chapter is intended to begin to close out this book with some takeaways from my work with the many teams I have been proudly associated with over my career. There are themes that relate mostly to discipline of taking responsibility in heart, mind and soul.

Living in the Basics like "Brushing your Teeth"

Prior to my time with Smile Brands, and working in the dental sector, I was using a metaphor from dental health with my team at Starbucks, a little irony. We were discussing ways to set concrete plans for store cleanliness and beverage standard execution using our tools. Under the mantra of "Living in the Basics" with job duties and building strong habits and repeatable routine I compared this to daily "brushing your teeth." And, once you start brushing, you will never stop because it becomes habit.

It's important to find fun and useful ways to get people rallied around daily discipline that may seem mundane and unexciting to the team at large. My cheesy way to describe this helped get the team joking, perhaps at my expense to execute basics of the business. Taking responsibility sometimes means getting the message sent in a self-deprecating way in using common language.

Understand by Asking "Why"

Teaching, coaching and developing people as a leader responsibility requires rich conversations and intense listening. The best learning comes from the people closest to the customer. Problem solving and sharing learning is how constant improvement is fostered. Taking responsibility for finding solutions and getting the message out is modeled by the leader.

At times, in program execution or customer transactions, shortcuts or unorthodox approaches take place. With this, store managers are usually at the dials of these "audibles." It is very important for the leader observing the deviation from standard to understand the reason behind the decision. It starts with "why."

At Starbucks, before automated cup labels, we emphasized the writing of names on cups by baristas as a key execution. We did so because 1) it eliminated confusion with multiple transactions and 2) it helped the barista to learn the name of the customer for friendly interaction from cash register to handoff (personalized service). In many cases, we found stores that failed to practice this consistently.

Asking "Why" would generally lead to a variety of responses. The following are the 3 key reasons we heard for not writing names on cups:

1. Forgot to ask
2. We know the customer and her drink
3. It has been busy, and we are shorthanded

"Forgot to Ask" is a mistake and acknowledgement that there is understanding of the standard. It gives the opportunity to reinforce the standard and expectation that it be executed. It also helps the dialogue to discuss ways avoid forgetting in the future.

"We know the customer and her drink" is intentional and maybe exceptional, but still not to standard. Unless the customer does not want her name on the cup, for whatever reason, not marking it leaves the opportunity for confusion. Asking why opens the door for good dialogue and improving execution.

The most disturbing response is "it has been busy, and we are shorthanded." Getting to the root cause problem here is multi-faceted. Why is the store shorthanded? Why is the standard abandoned in busy periods? Inside of those questions are likely several more to peel back the onion and help the team and customers. Asking "why" is taking responsibility to serve others and create learning for individuals and the team.

Taking Responsibility for "Asking Why"

Key Takeaways:
- ✓ *Strategy:* Teaching, coaching and development culture through curiosity and emphasis on "asking why."
- ✓ *Basic:* Asking "why" is problem-solving and listening to people close to customer.
- ✓ *Execution:* Leader constantly asking "why" enables peeling back the onion to improve and reinforce and to infuse the behavior to team.

Focus on Communication

Taking responsibility in heart, mind and soul requires frequent and impactful communication with the leader individually and as a team. Formal communication as a team should happen weekly by phone and monthly or quarterly in person. Meetings should have an agenda that is published in advance with participation in the meeting required by all attending. The best meetings are interactive with takeaway actions on key priorities to help and serve the team and customers.

Individual meetings are best while attending to the normal course of business with store visits or other customer focused activity. It creates a reality check and opportunity for discussion of ways to elevate personally or as a team working with the leader. The goal of individual meetings should be relationship development, addressing individual development and performance feedback. Taking responsibility should always have a completely open-door policy of communication.

Taking Responsibility for Focus on Communication

Key Takeaways:
- ✓ *Strategy:* Routine communication process supports a functional work team.
- ✓ *Execution:* Implement a routine weekly, monthly formal communication process with the team.
- ✓ *Execution:* Make meetings interactive with takeaway actions.
- ✓ *Execution:* Focus individual meetings on serving the individual.

<u>Open, Honest and Doing the "Right Thing"</u>

Taking responsibility is doing the "right thing." Reinforcing an environment of openness and acknowledging challenges welcomes support and help to elevate. The word transparency maybe overused in today's world, but it is important to be ethical with an eye on fairness and serving others. At times, the truth is brutal. However, when the brutal facts are clear, even in the face of disastrous results, the problem-solving actions should be thoughtfully considered and implemented.

A culture of taking responsibility in heart, mind and soul is lined with high ethics. Many times, in business and organizations, poor decisions are made for short-term and often self-serving financial gain. This is "looking good" not "being good." It is also dishonest and robs the people in the organization of confronting and learning from adversity to sustain long term values that lead to a high performing organization. Decision-making should be considerate of a healthy culture led by responsible people.

Taking Responsibility for being Open, Honest and Doing the "Right Thing"

Key Takeaways:
- ✓ *Strategy:* Culture lined with high ethics.
- ✓ *Basic:* Poor decisions often come from short term and self-serving motives.
- ✓ *Execution:* Confront and learn from adversity, obstacles and poor ethical decisions.
- ✓ *Execution:* Leader frequently describes what high ethics mean and invites dialogue.

Urgently Confront Obstacles and Adversity

Taking responsibility often means the leader is not one to "let the grass grow under her/his feet." Obstacles and adversity occur often in any business or organization. When facing issues and adversity in taking action to achieve strong performance, growth and results, it is crucial that there is a sense of urgency. This means the leader must understand the obstacles, communicate openly with the team and set direction to address the problems effectively. This requires appropriate timeframes and report backs to assess that progress and resolution is achieved.

A strong sense of urgency to deal with adversity often prevents smaller obstacles from growing into full-blown problems that put an initiative at risk. The leader has the responsibility to be vigilant and foresee pitfalls before they occur. Through functional and healthy communication between the leader and the team, adversity can be addressed and even avoided. This is fundamental to the *Tanpin Kanri* process discussed in chapter four.

Taking Responsibility to Urgently Confront Obstacles and Adversity

Key Takeaways:
- ✓ *Strategy:* Culturally reinforce the notion of sense of urgency and effective problem solving.
- ✓ *Execution:* Don't "let the grass grow under... feet" in dealing with adversity.
- ✓ *Execution:* Be vigilant and foresee pitfalls before they occur by using examples and specifics from past and red flags.

Use Facts to Drive Action

Too often in business and organizations, leaders are swept up by great sounding ideas that are short on actual learning or specific facts to substantiate potential. This is not to say that great ideas and even dreams aren't important to change a trend to achieve growth objectives. In fact these could be game changers. However, the leader has the responsibility to require examples, learnings, testing and models to prove a reasonable shot of success. By taking this responsibility, the leader pushes the team to use the four-step process of *Tanpin Kanri* to have discipline in decision making. Good decisions are enhanced by rigor.

Taking Responsibility Use Facts to Drive Action

Key Takeaways:
- ✓ *Strategy:* Culturally inspire proper analysis in problem solving.
- ✓ *Execution:* Use the four-step process of *Tanpin Kanri* to make important decisions.

Deny the Status Quo

"We have always done it this way." This is something most of us have heard in working with large organizations. Change is difficult but change is the lifeblood of sustaining growth in business and organizations. Resisting and denying the status quo is a key part of *Tanpin Kanri* and, more importantly, the way new ideas are welcomed and fostered to prosper. Denying the Status Quo is the responsibility of the leader to make it real in the culture.

The "art" of leading change is ensuring that the great

longstanding practices and programs are preserved, while incorporating modifications and new products or services. Starbucks is an example of an organization that has accomplished and continues to accomplish customer focused change effectively. The brand continues to be World Class while new approaches like mobile ordering are successfully implemented in 20,000 stores.

Taking Responsibility to Deny the Status Quo

Key Takeaways:
- ✓ *Strategy:* Make denying the status quo real in the culture.
- ✓ *Execution:* Preserve longstanding practices and programs while making constant modifications in new products and services.

"Raising the Bar" Mindset

The Leader has the responsibility for "never settling" with regard to performance and success of the team and the organization. Too often leaders tend to rely on past success stories where they "read their own press clippings." Celebrate a win and pat the individual or team on the back for great work and move on to more improvement. For the good of the team the leader must have sustained performance as the grand focus. This is crucial to a performance culture while serving others.

Taking Responsibility for a "Raising the Bar" Mindset

Key Takeaways:
- ✓ *Strategy:* Reinforce a mindset of a performance culture
- ✓ *Execution:* Celebrate wins and move on to more improvement

Epilogue

Taking Responsibility: Heart, Mind and Soul

The meaning and message of this writing relates to selflessness, caring and considering others in work and life as a responsible individual. When called upon, or when seeking to lead others to help them overcome obstacles and succeed at important missions and tasks, it is never being "me" first.

Taking responsibility as a parent, a sibling, a boss, a colleague, a friend, a coach or a teacher is most successful when every piece of your being is exercised in heart, mind and soul.

Taking responsibility in heart, mind and soul is rejecting being a victim under any circumstance. This is a forward-looking sense of being in finding solutions and options to adversity while helping others do the same. It is a problem-solving mindset that begins with the end in mind and finding a path to success.

Taking responsibility in heart, mind and soul is about being relentless and determined to achieve goals and help others with a roadmap to succeed. This is a "give it all" mindset that creates energy and inspiration.

Taking responsibility in heart, mind and soul is about being a consummate professional. A professional is competent, works hard, is reliable to leaders and colleagues, has a confident composure and performs well even when he/she does not feel like it.

Taking responsibility in heart, mind and soul is about serving others. It is taking joy in serving and helping others succeed or overcoming adversity. This provides the energy and tone in leading a team.

Taking responsibility in heart, mind and soul requires high character and ethics. It is honesty and transparency with individuals and with audiences of all sizes, unafraid of the facts and the truth.

Thank You, Jeff

Acknowledgements

First and foremost, thanks to my wife Kathy for the loving encouragement and support all along the way with this project. Her reading and comments throughout were motivation to get this book to the finish line.

Special thanks to Mark Lindstrom for writing the foreword of this book. His incredible leadership and impact on my career and perspective is instrumental to the message.

Also, special thanks to the editor, Janice Hamill for providing exceptional editing support. Her professional guidance and assistance greatly enhanced the message and readability.

Thanks to my brother Steve for once again encouraging me to be uncomfortable and head down a road I haven't taken before. As always, his caring guidance enriches my endeavors.

Thanks to my brother Bill for his energetic encouragement and rich feedback to improve the work product dramatically. The enhancements are pivotal to the message of the book.

Thanks to my son Dan for his knowledge of business leadership and providing important feedback to improve the book using his keen insights. His smart skills have provided practical enhancements.

Thanks to my daughter Britt for the technical writing skill support and getting me to the proper place to publish – no small task. She snuck in valuable insights while attending to 2 kids under 3!

Thanks to my nephew Chad Hamill, successful author and college professor for his insightful guidance early on in the project. His experienced assistance was invaluable to help me connect with the reader.

Thanks to my brother Jim for his encouraging words of support of the project. His belief in me is one more confidence builder in a long line he has provided over my life.

Thanks to my good friend Miguel Foegal for his excellent insights and suggestions to make this the best book it could be.

All of these key people are part of the imprint that created Taking Responsibility: Heart, Mind and Soul.

Joy and Pride

My overwhelming joy is the pride I have in my family-my 40-year marriage to Kathy and our loving partnership that brought us 2 outstanding offspring. Dan was born in 1981 and Brittany born in 1985. Kathy is like an angel from heaven in my life. There is no such thing as a perfect relationship or marriage, but we have overcome the serious obstacles many married people face, and we have only strengthened in our commitment to each other and to our family. We have unconditional love for one another and acknowledge that fact daily, by the actions we take, not just the words we say to one another.

When I was diagnosed with stage four lymphoma in 2007, Kathy took on an unselfish and unwavering support of me that was extraordinary. All the treatments, surgery and stressful uncertainty surrounding that cancer required strong faith and hope. She was at my side at every juncture over a period of years, fighting this thing. Though, I have never been closer to anyone else on the planet, the cancer strangely unveiled an enhanced level of heart, mind and soul from Kathy. I was able to experience unconditional love with the extreme acts of kindness. It was unforgettable and I will be eternally grateful for this and her daily love.

Dan, born in 1981, is a smart, talented and hard-working man that was diligent to complete his business degree in 4 years at UC Riverside, immediately following high school, and his master's degree at USF thereafter. He has worked in the beverage sales and distribution business for 16 years since college and, at age 38, is now the Vice President of Commercial Sales for Golden Road Brewing in Los Angeles. Dan worked for Anheuser Busch for 12 years before he joined Golden Road, a craft brewer, that was purchased by AB after Dan joined.

Dan married Emily in 2011 and they own a home in Los Angeles. His future and Emily's future, who also has a great career in business, is very bright due to their focus, career goals and business achievements. My joy and pride are that Dan embraces responsibility and constantly elevates in his work, life and marriage to Emily. It is clear they have created a great life together.

Dan has taken responsibility in heart, mind and soul, for his education and his blossoming career. He has always been a great student, a hard worker and has been well-regarded by his companies and bosses along the way. At times, I have coached and helped him, like most dads would, but he has been a very willing listener and participant. Dan has made many very good career decisions on his own. I am very proud of his sense of responsibility and achievements at a young age in the competitive business world.

Dan and I stay connected though we now live 500 miles apart. We are both NFL fans and have season tickets to the LA Rams games. I travel from the Bay Area to Southern California for each home game. It is very important to me that I have a strong bond with Dan and get the pleasure of being a part of his life in a real way in heart, mind and soul. I am overwhelmingly proud to be Dan's Dad.

Brittany, born in 1985, is a bright, resourceful and diligent woman that completed her undergraduate studies at UCLA, immediately following high school. She completed her graduate teaching credential studies at Cal State Long Beach immediately thereafter. Britt spent several years at a very special elementary school in Newhall, California teaching sixth grade to an underprivileged population of kids – many with English as a second language. Britt's tender heart and love for children is special. I marvel at the love and compassion she has for her family, her friends and really anyone she touches, like her students at McGrath Elementary in Newhall.

Britt married Brandon in 2013 and has 2 children, our grandkids- Luke and Camryn (joy and pride!). Her husband Brandon, an attorney, has known her since they both attended UCLA, and they operate as a great team of parents. Recently, we returned home to the

Bay Area where Brittany and Brandon live and where it all started for Kathy and me over 40 years ago. It is great to be part of the process with Luke and Camryn. We both love our grandkids and this new life is bringing great joy.

Britt is very special to me. As I spoke at her wedding, I related that I have 3 brothers and a son before she was born. When around girls I never quite "got it" until she arrived. She taught me more about relating to females than I ever knew, and she did it without knowing it. She has taken responsibility for her family and her life in heart, mind and soul. Britt has always been an exceptional student, an outstanding teacher and now a loving and nurturing mom. I am extremely proud of her achievements and the loving heart that is always on display.

My family is the reason and purpose for everything I have done on this planet and in my life the last 40 years. The demands related to the work and positions I held over my career were significant in the many hours of travel each day and the distractions that come with the territory. However, taking responsibility with heart, mind and soul enabled the joy and pride. I am very thankful for my beautiful and special family. In order to be great at work it is necessary to be great at home for true fulfillment in heart, mind and soul.

Thanks again, Jeff

References

Autry, James A. *The Servant Leader*. New York: Three Rivers Press, 2001.

Ball, David and Hal Hogan. "Tanpin Kanri: Retail Practice at Seven-Eleven Japan." Harvard Business School Case 504-057, January 2004.

Buckingham, Marcus and David Clifton. *Now, Discover Your Strengths*. New York: The Free Press, 2001.

Collins, Jim. *Good to Great*. New York: Harper Collins, 2001.

Hersey, Dr. Paul. *The Situational Leader*. New York: Warner Books, 1985.

Powell, Colin. "A Leadership Primer." Outreach to America Program, 1997, Sears Corporate HQ, Chicago, IL. Briefing.

JH Leadership – Jeffrey Hamill
Website jhleadership.com to arrange workshops

www.ingramcontent.com/pod-product-compliance
Lightning Source LLC
Chambersburg PA
CBHW021957170526
45157CB00003B/1025